FANTASY DRESSED ANIMALS

Brian W. Parker

Edited by Sean Fishback

Book designed and illustration by Brian W. Parker, BFA, MA
Edited by Sean Fishback
Inside text set in Felix Tiling and Danielle
BIW "reading boy" logo is a trademark of Believe In Wonder Publishing, LLC

Printed in the U.S.A
For bulk orders, event booking, and questions about publishing services,
please email us at believeinwonderpublishing@gmail.com

ISBN: 9781795888776

BISAC: Art / Individual Artists / Artists Books

First Edition

Summary: Author and illustrator, Brian W. Parker, proudly brings together
a second collection of skillfully executed pencil drawings depicting a menagerie of animals in fantasy settings and attire.

Believe In Wonder is a family-owned, youth focused publishing company
based in Beaverton, OR. We delight in promoting imagination, inspiration,
and positive thinking in kids and adults alike, and strive to bring diverse characters and new worlds to readers and art lovers everywhere.

Visit us at **believeinwonder.com** for more books, art, and event updates.

FANTASY
DRESSED
ANIMALS

A collection of illustrations by Brian W. Parker

CONTAINING:
Golden tiger, platypus, Kodiak bear, fennec fox, river otter,
and a menagerie of other varied beasts in fantasy settings.

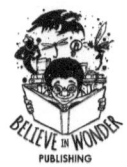

PUBLISHING

BEAVERTON • OREGON

"Wonder is the beginning of wisdom."
-Socrates

for the students of Evergreen Middle School

Thank you for always inspiring me.

An introduction

Ever since I can remember, I have loved coming up with characters. I would imagine them in far off lands, on grand adventures, and solving incredible mysteries. These characters were as much a part of my childhood as any real event that ever happened to me. I learned how to draw and write stories so I could share those characters with other people. That's what this book is. This is me sharing my love of characters with you.

Thank you so much.

Sir Edgar Burrows

Knight of the High Oak

Edgar lost his family to the Skulking Horde when he was barely a cub and found himself alone in the world. Luckily he was found by an unexpected benefactor - Zontos the Wise, the wandering knight from the east. The elder fox took the young badger as his ward, and though he was angry and headstrong Zontos saw greatness in Edgar's dark eyes. They traveled the Woodland together helping the poor and powerless, and in time Edgar defined his life by service to those in need. Even though he was not high born, the creatures of the Woodland began to call him Sir Edgar, Knight of the High Oak.

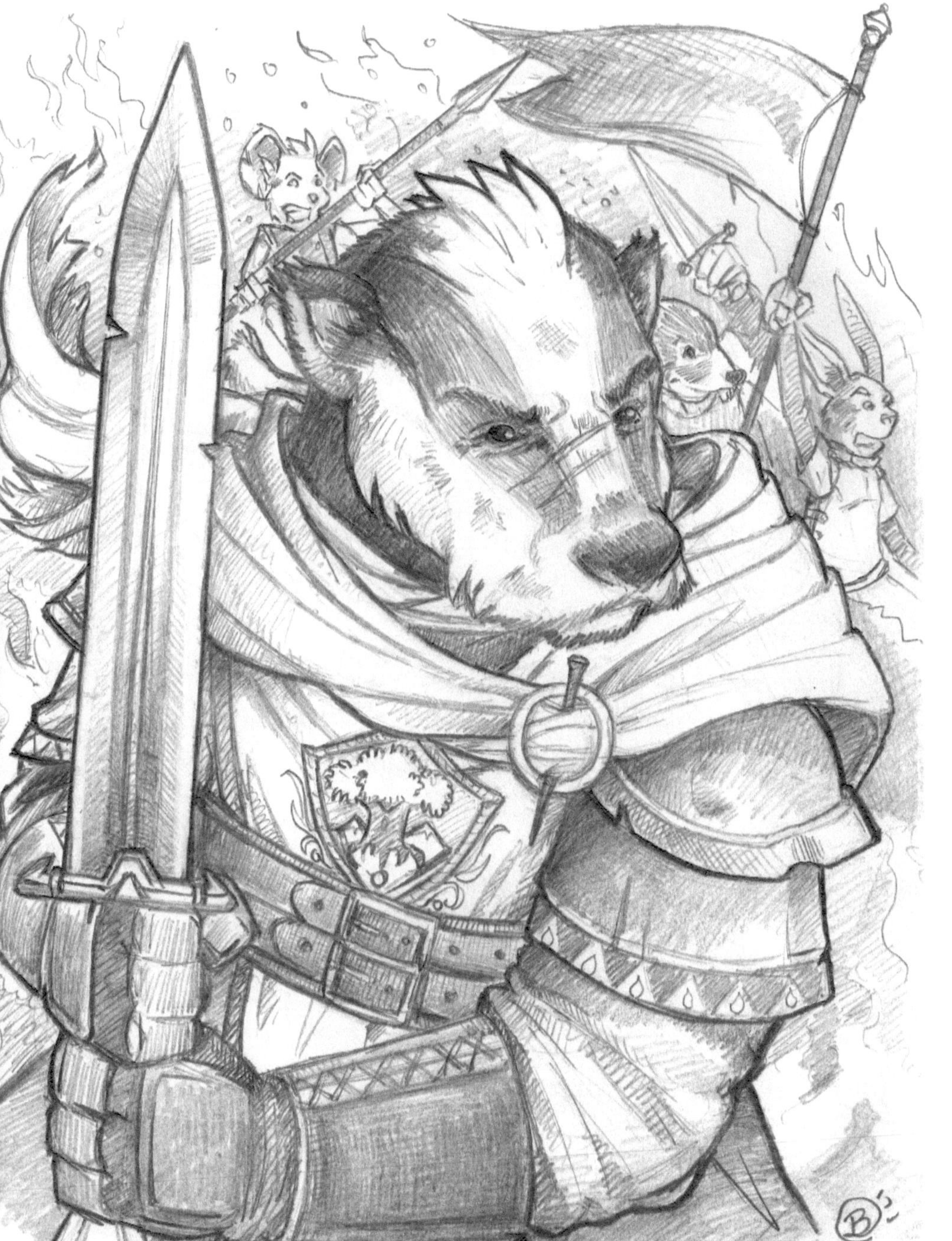

Ainia

Battle Priestess of the Hidden Glade

Few creatures travel through the Hidden Glade, and fewer still have faced the fighting prowess of the priestesses that dwell there and lived to tell the tale. Their spears are sharp, their arms strong, and their speed unmatched by any beast. Many secrets lie within the tall grass of the glade, shrouded in mist and mystery. As long as the priestesses draw breath, it will stay that way.

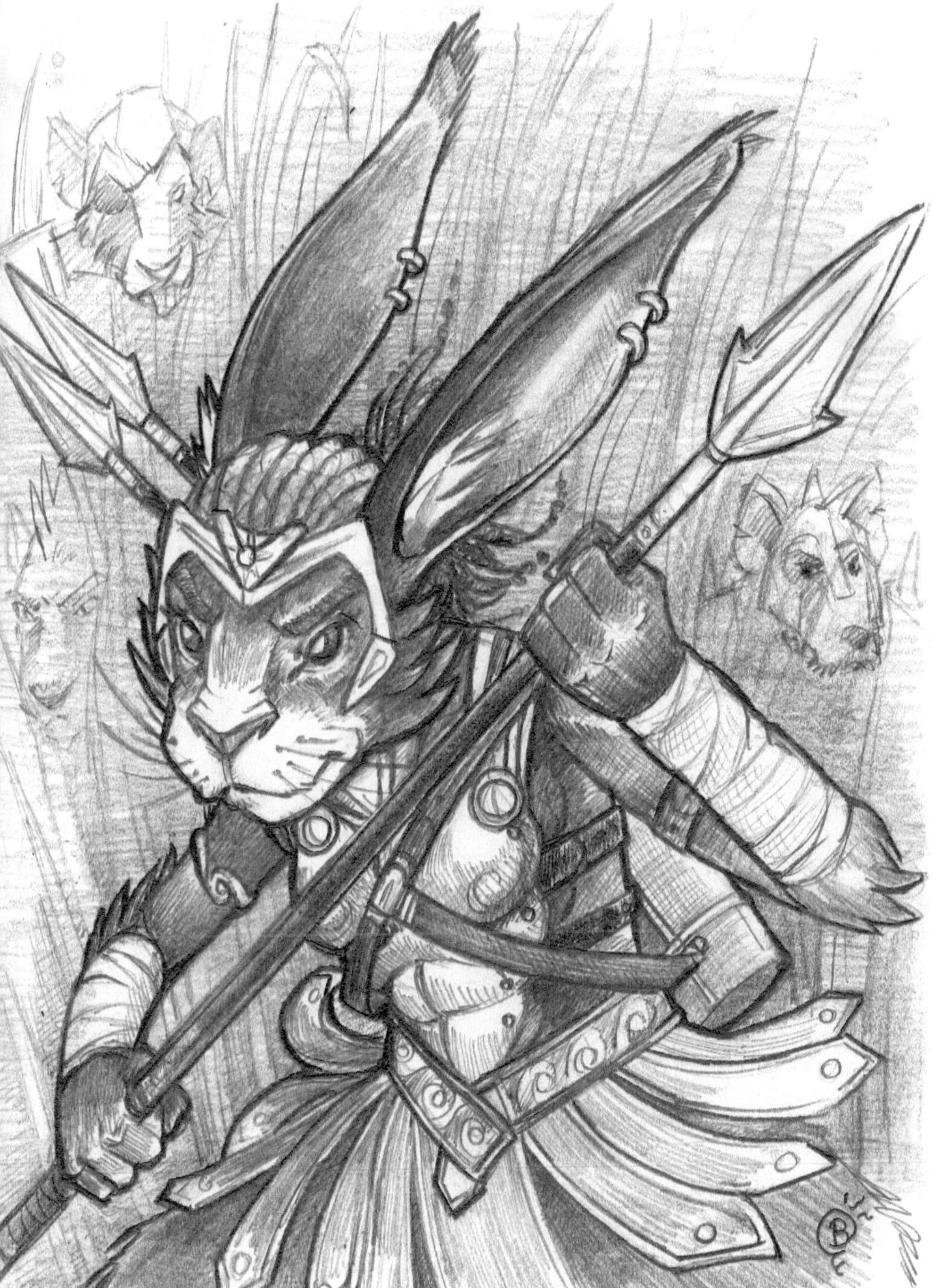

Rand August

The Red Sorcerer

Rand doesn't seek out trouble, but somehow it always seems to find him. Be it a little tavern fight over a questionable hand of cards, or a full-on battle with a cadre of bear folk, this red panda is no stranger to danger. He's a regular member of adventuring parties, and an old hand at fighting off giant spiders, zombies, and skeletons that stand in the way of treasure. Even though he's known for getting into high-risk situations, he has a well-earned reputation for getting out of them.

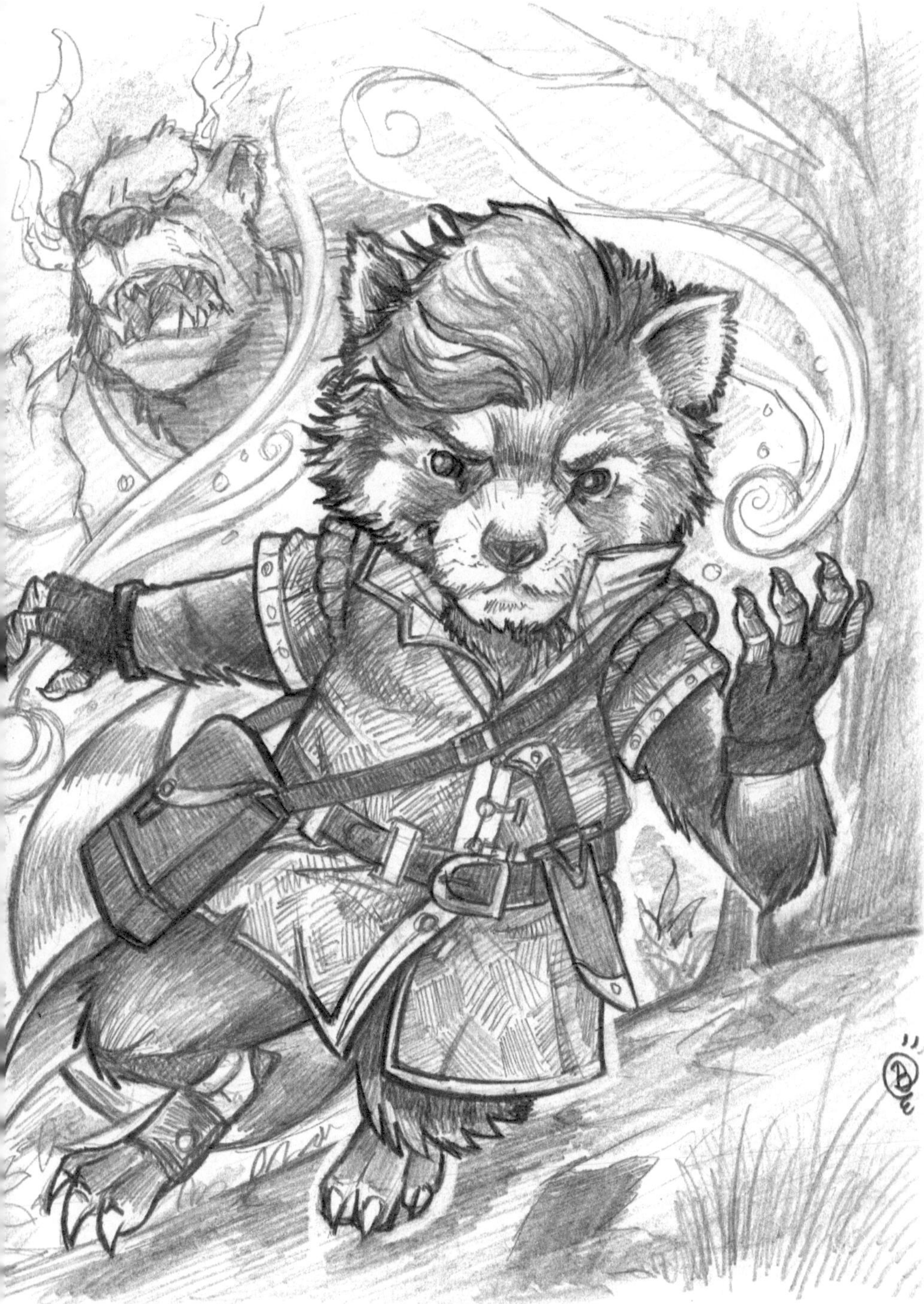

Jorge Cavia

The Head Smasher

He may be small, but Jorge Cavia packs a punch. Raised in a traveling circus, Jorge dreamed of someday becoming the star attraction instead of a roustabout like his father. He spent everyday with anyone that would train him, from the tumbling team to the legendary strongman, El Jefe. It wasn't until the summer that the circus was attacked by the Skulking Horde that Jorge found his true calling - he was a brawler. He fought off the Horde minions, using his small size, tumbling skills and unexpected strength to his advantage. He saved his traveling family and earned the name The Head Smasher.

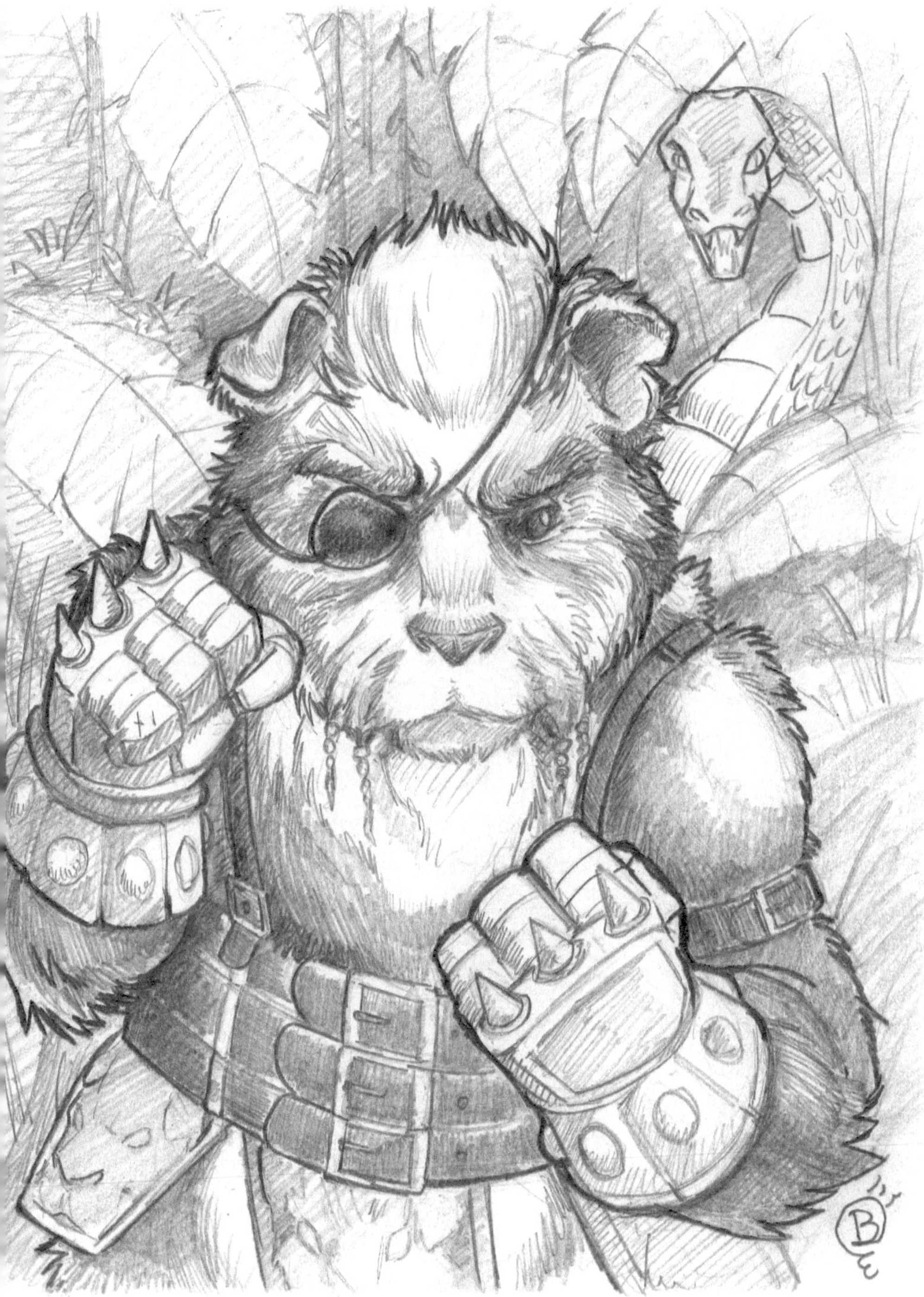

Ohasis Eben Tut

the Hermit

The Order of the Silver Pool is an ancient group of mages. Their powers of precognition are legendary, and the Oracle of the Silver Pool is their matron. Ohasis, however, is a little different than his brethren. Instead of watching as the future unfolds, aloof and detached, he is driven to act. He uses his knowledge to help those in need. Despite the objections of his order, he has gotten quite good at it. Nothing is more confusing to an evil-doer than having a turtle monk show up BEFORE you do evil.

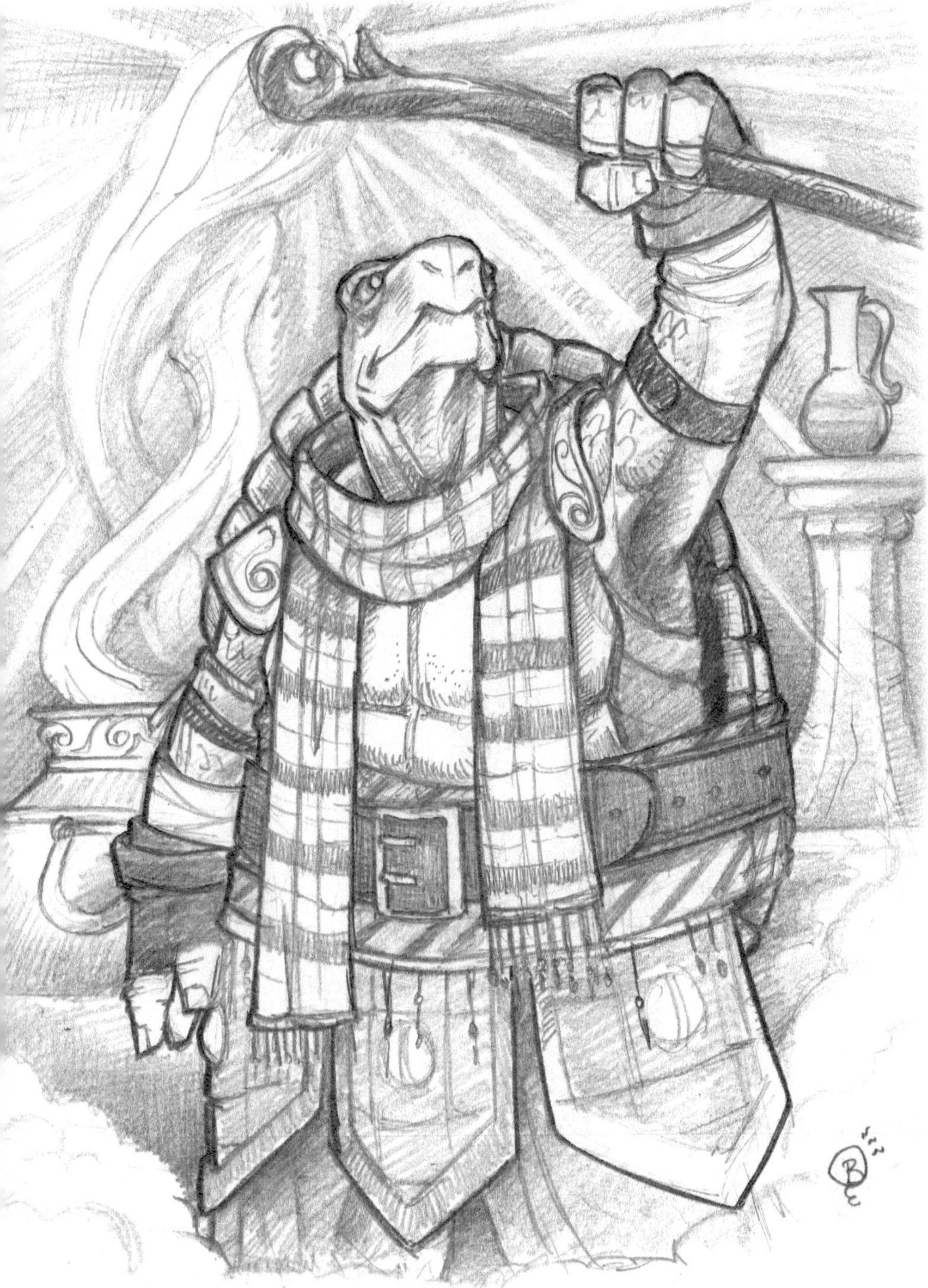

Galen Blutpeltz

The Woodland Archer

The Woodland can be a dangerous place. There are dark hollows where eyes stare out from the shadows filled with hunger and malice. But never fear. If you are a peace-loving beast, you will always have a friend watching your back. Galen Blutpeltz watches the trails that crisscross the forest, keeping his keen eyes on the lookout for bandits and cutthroats of all kinds. When evil strikes, his arrows fly fast and true.

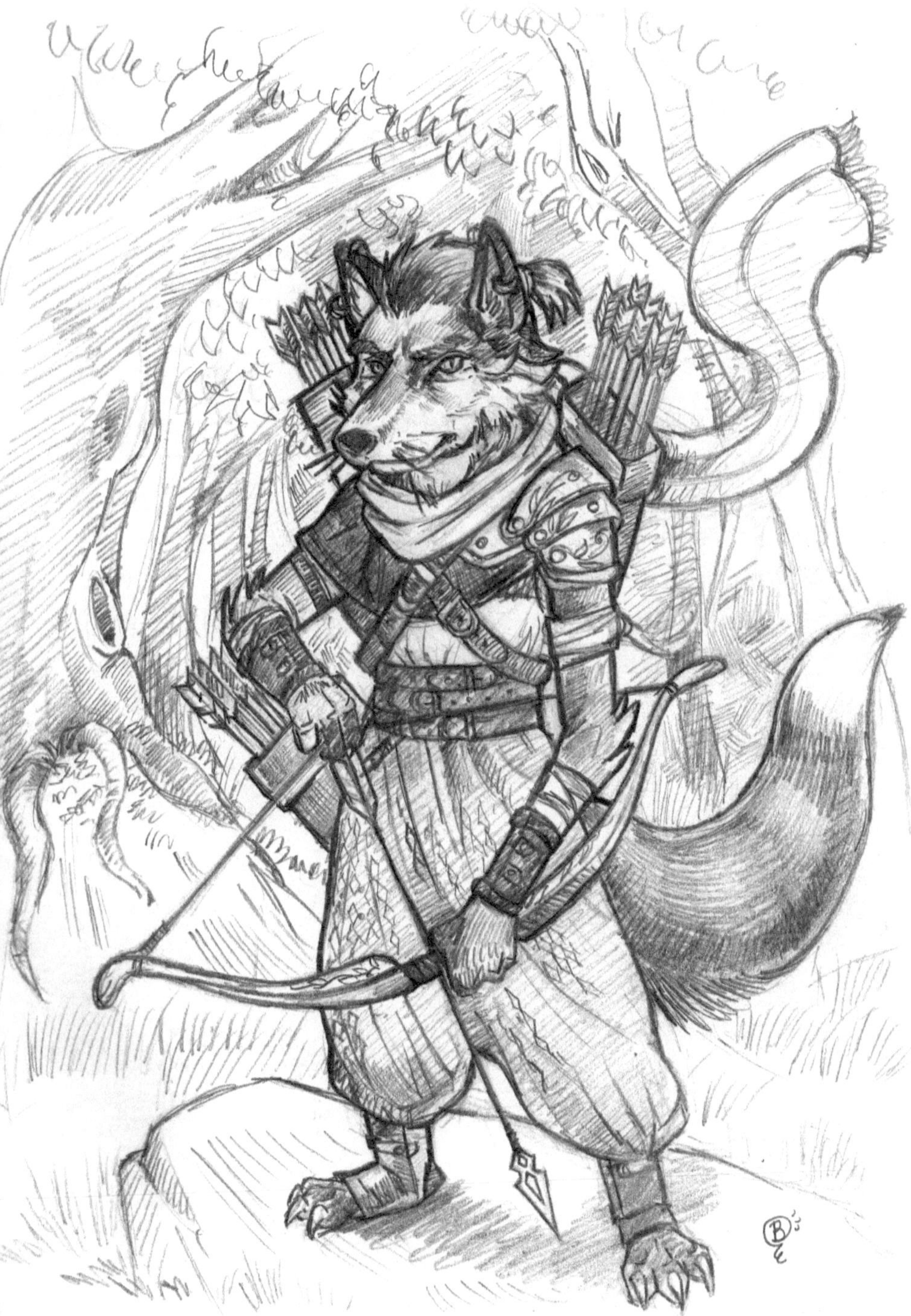

Li Xing Fu

Master of The Iron Weasel

The docks belong to the Hatchet Gang, everybody knows that. Nothing comes in or out of town without them getting their cut. Apparently, no one told Li Xing Fu. Never stand in the way of a master of iron weasel kung fu when he's determined to deal out justice. His strikes are precise, his will is tenacious, and his fists are unstoppable.

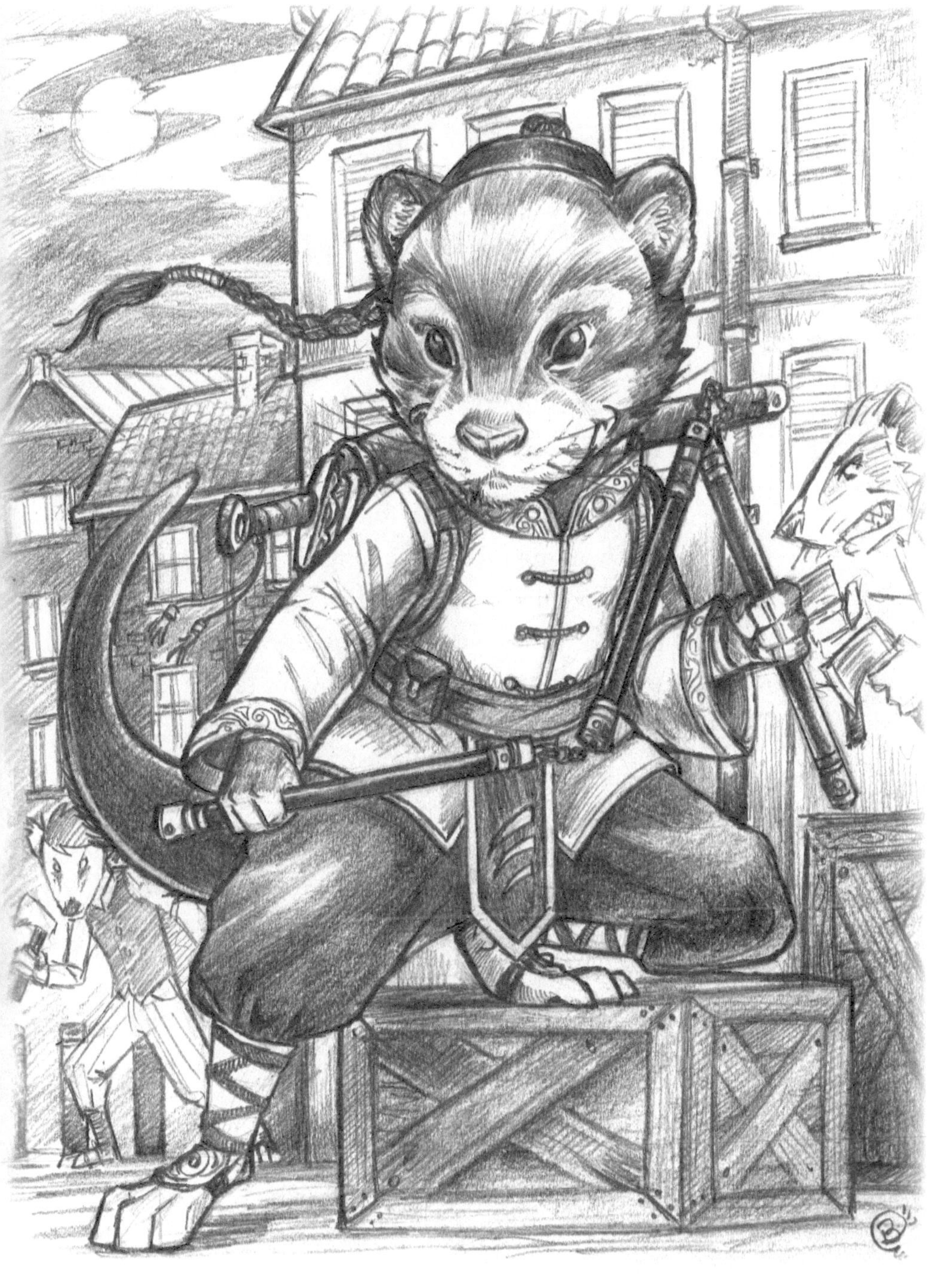

Mordecai E. Roquefort

Grave Robber Extraordinaire

Mordecai has never been known for his "respectability." After years of working for the Skulking Horde as a low-level thug, he decided to give up the life of pillaging and skip straight to the getting-paid part. So began a life of stealing from the dead. "If they want tombs left alone, then why put treasure in them?" he said right before stealing the golden mask of Imrohan the Great (and subsequently unleashing his thousand-year-old mummy in the process.)

Tomb raiding is a messy business.

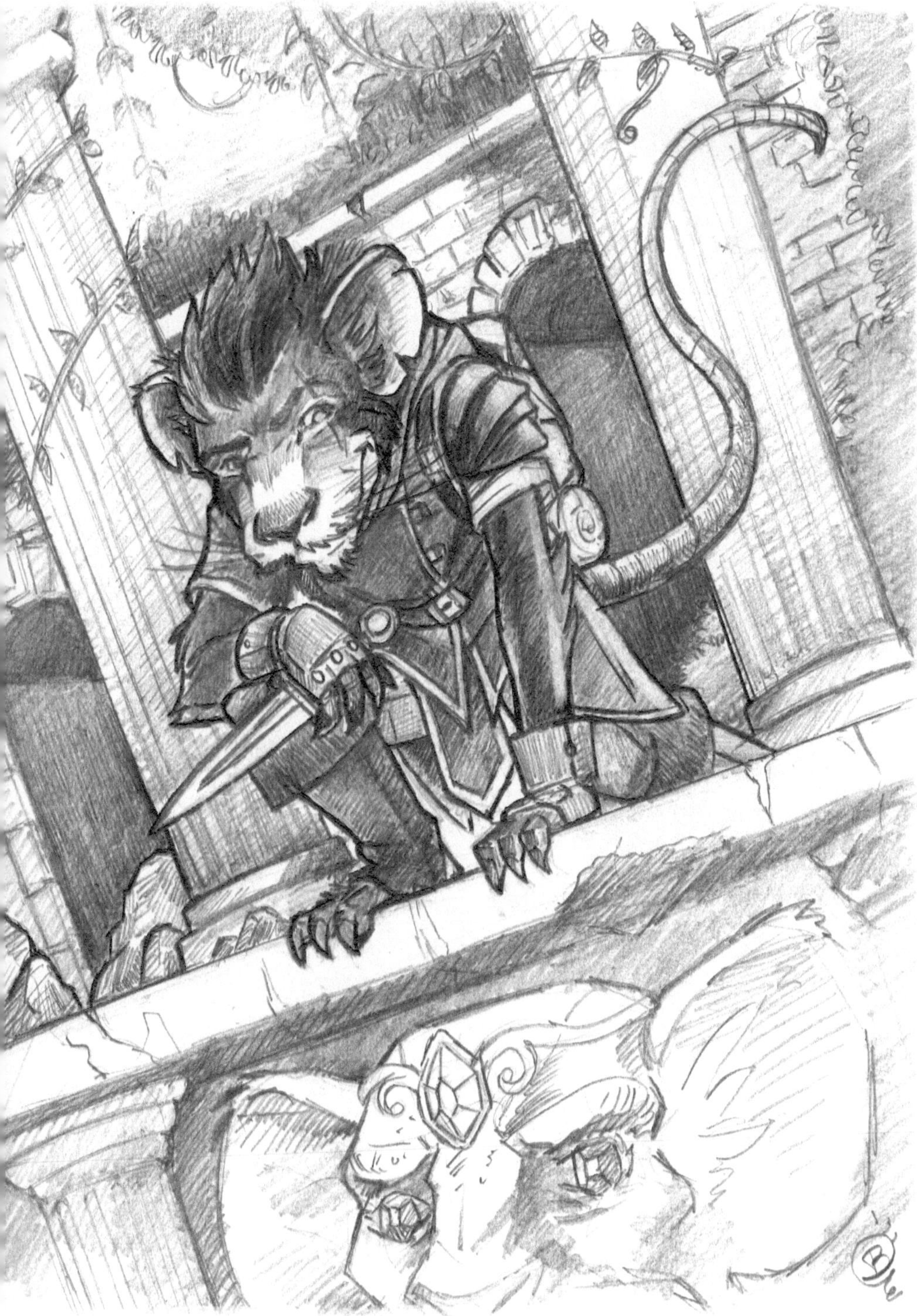

Magos

Son of Marhabal the Bold

You can hear their thunderous march across the savannah, moving with steady force, strength, and determination. The rhinos of Cannahal are a military machine with one true cause - to conquer. At the head of their ranks stands Magos the Indomitable; Magos the Terrible; Magos the Unyielding. Like his father before him, he holds his great hammer in weathered hands and dreams of the battlefields that lay beyond the horizon.

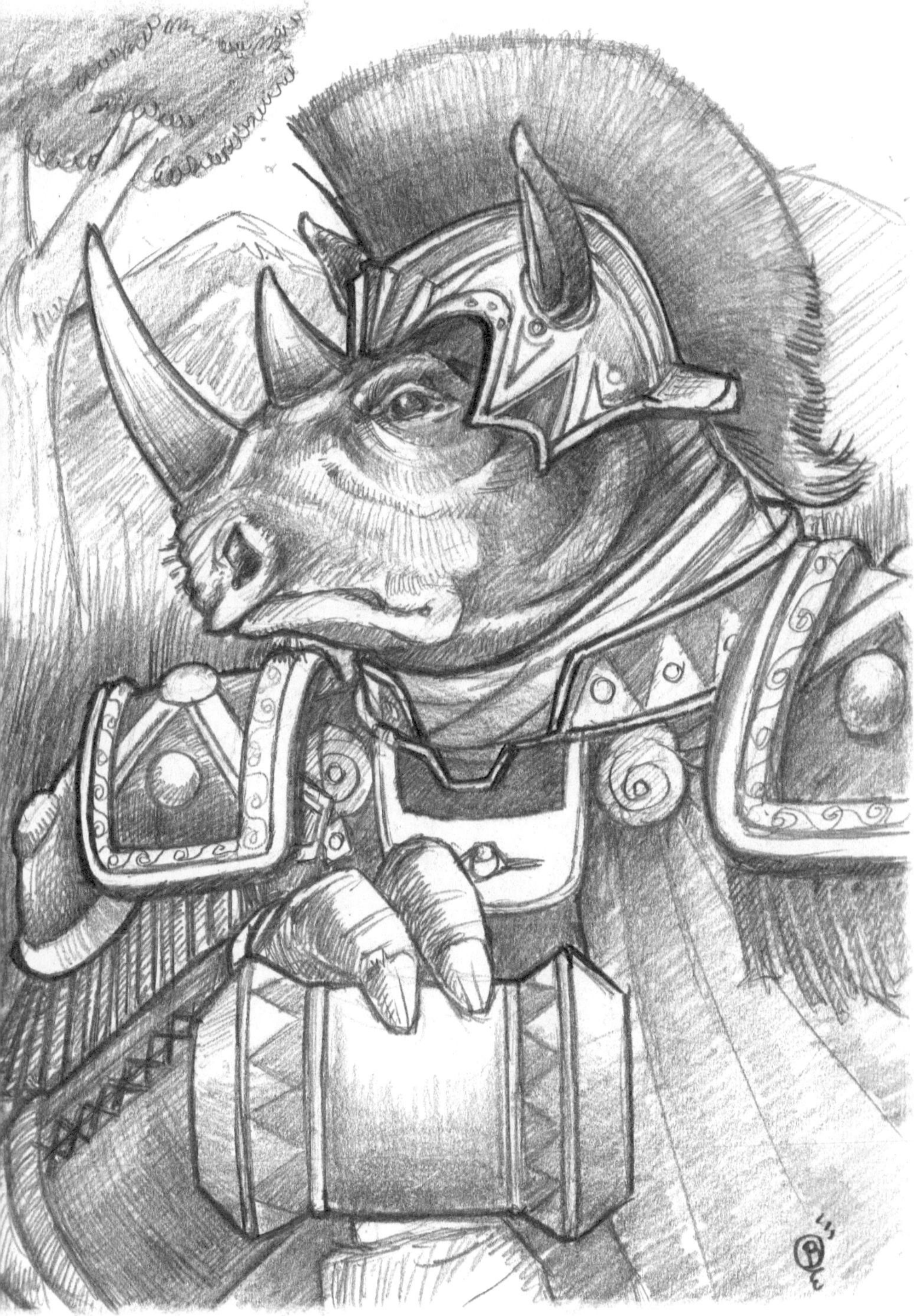

Rhy Yantell

High Cleric of the Stygian Monastery

High in the craggy foothills of Mount Darkholme lie the Stygian Caverns. The labyrinthian depths hold many dangers, but to the determined seeker there are secrets to be discovered. A monastic order has built their home in these stony passages, carved deep into the dark slate. You can hear their chants resonating through the caves as they perform their ancient rites. Their purpose is as mysterious as their leader, Rhy Yantell, but it is said that he holds the very secrets of life and death.

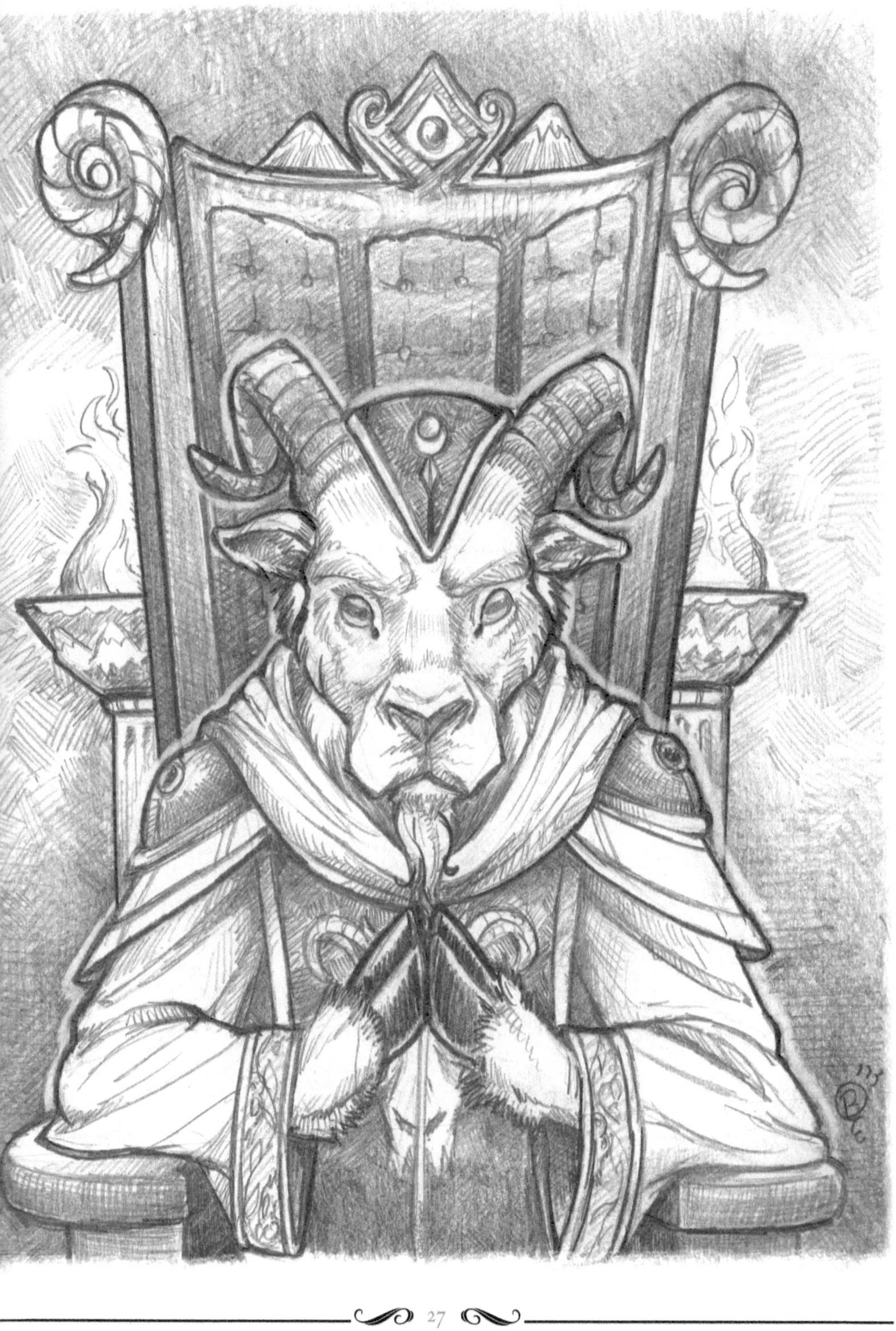

Boldebar the Strong

First of His Name

Woe to those unfortunate enough to face the clans of Ebenwald. These nomadic warrior-boar live deep in the tangled Woodland, fighting amongst themselves for territory. Boldebar rose up from the tribal conflict and has a legitimate chance of bringing the clans together. Once he does, woe to the enemies of a unified Ebenwald.

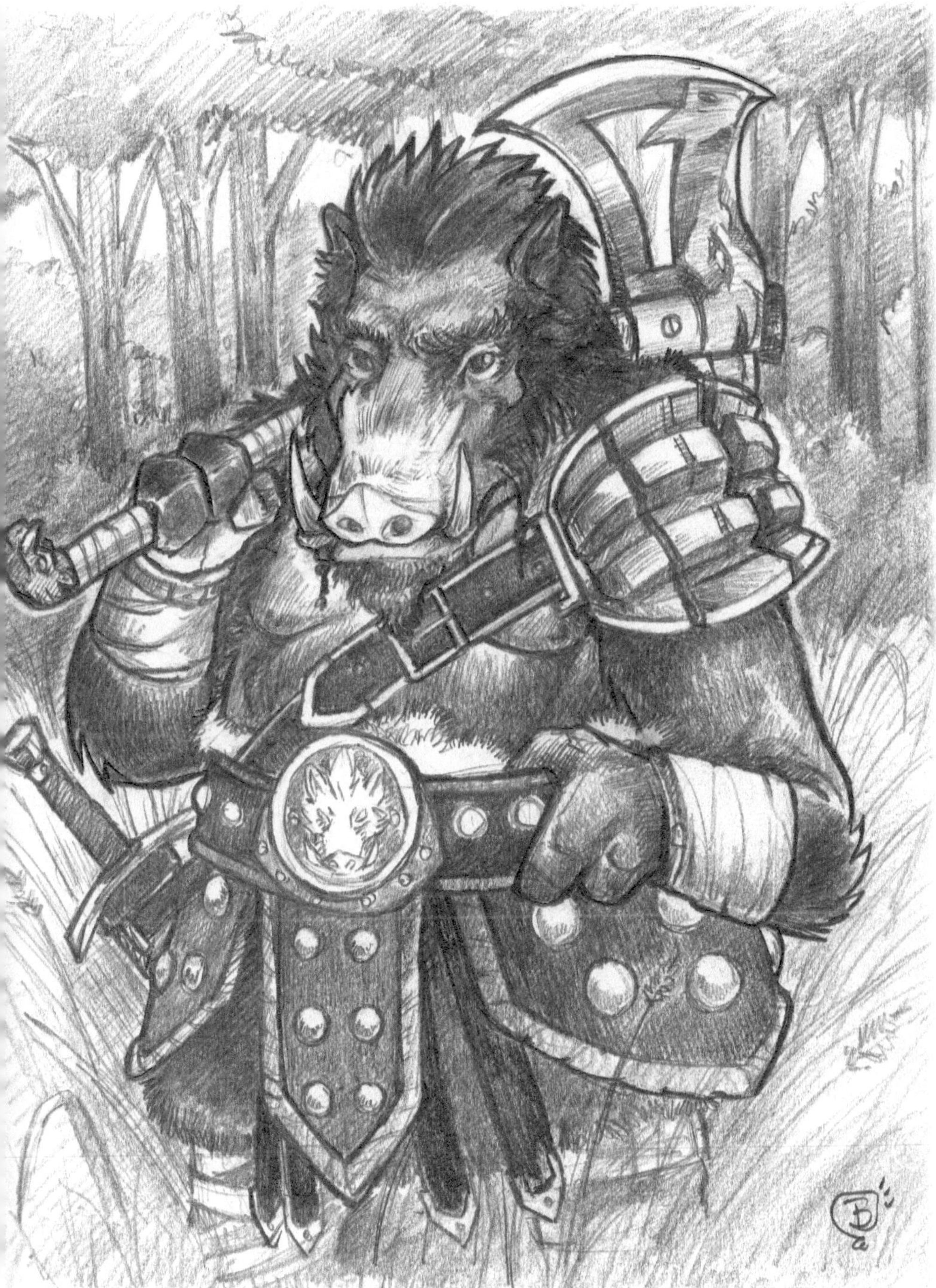

Kolan Kan-demir

Sentinel of the White Tower

Kolan is a paragon of knightly virtue. He has protected the royal family since he ascended to the role of tower sentinel at only seventeen, and given the high honor of being the personal guard to the next in line to the Snowy Thrown, Princess Invisha. He's respected by the other sentinels of the palace and held in high esteem by the aristocracy. That high opinion, however, might change once they learn his secret - Kolan Kan-demir is in love with the princess he is sworn to protect. Even more scandalous, she's in love with him.

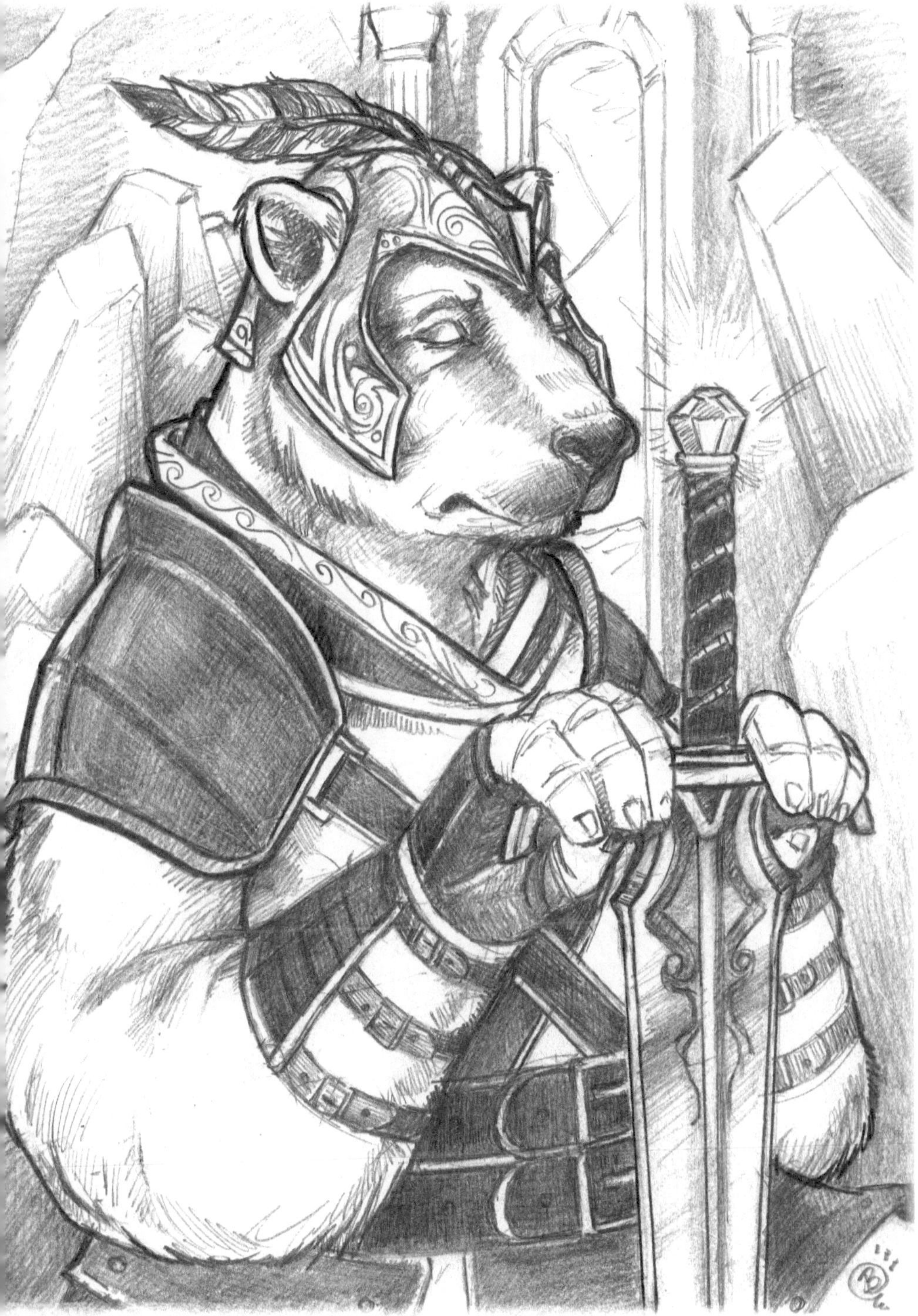

Sun Wukong

The Monkey King

The Monkey King's legend has grown throughout the centuries, as has his knowledge and power. Few beasts will ever achieve his strength, but that doesn't stop them from testing that fact. Sun Wukong wouldn't have it any other way.

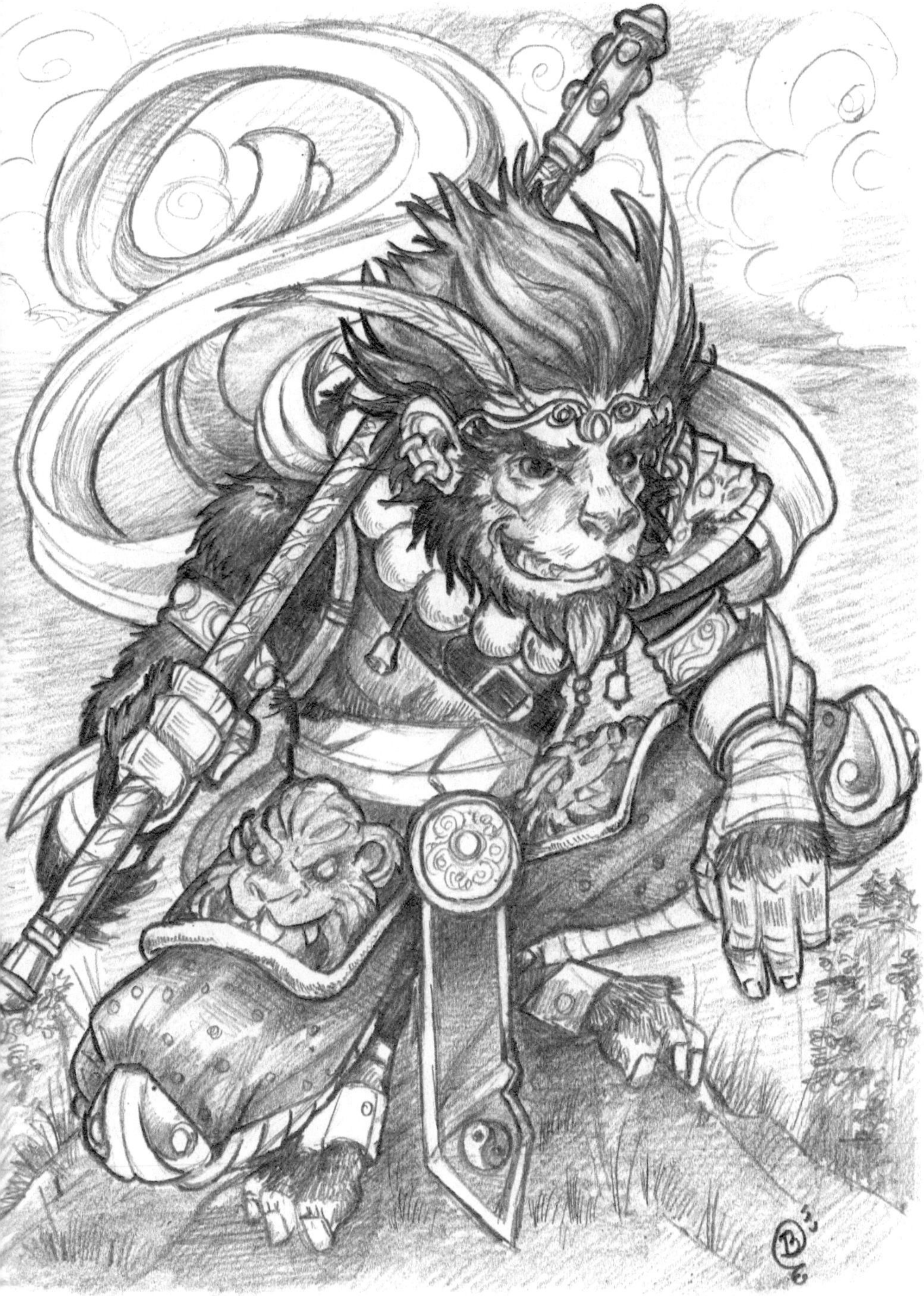

Zhang Bao

Soldier of the Wu Shen Dynasty

Bao never wanted to go to war. He was content with his work as a simple blacksmith, but when the emperor's call went out he answered. His village sat on the western border, and when the hordes of Ebenwald came they ruthlessly tore across the farmlands. He wasn't content to just make armor and swords. To defend his home, he was determined to use them as well.

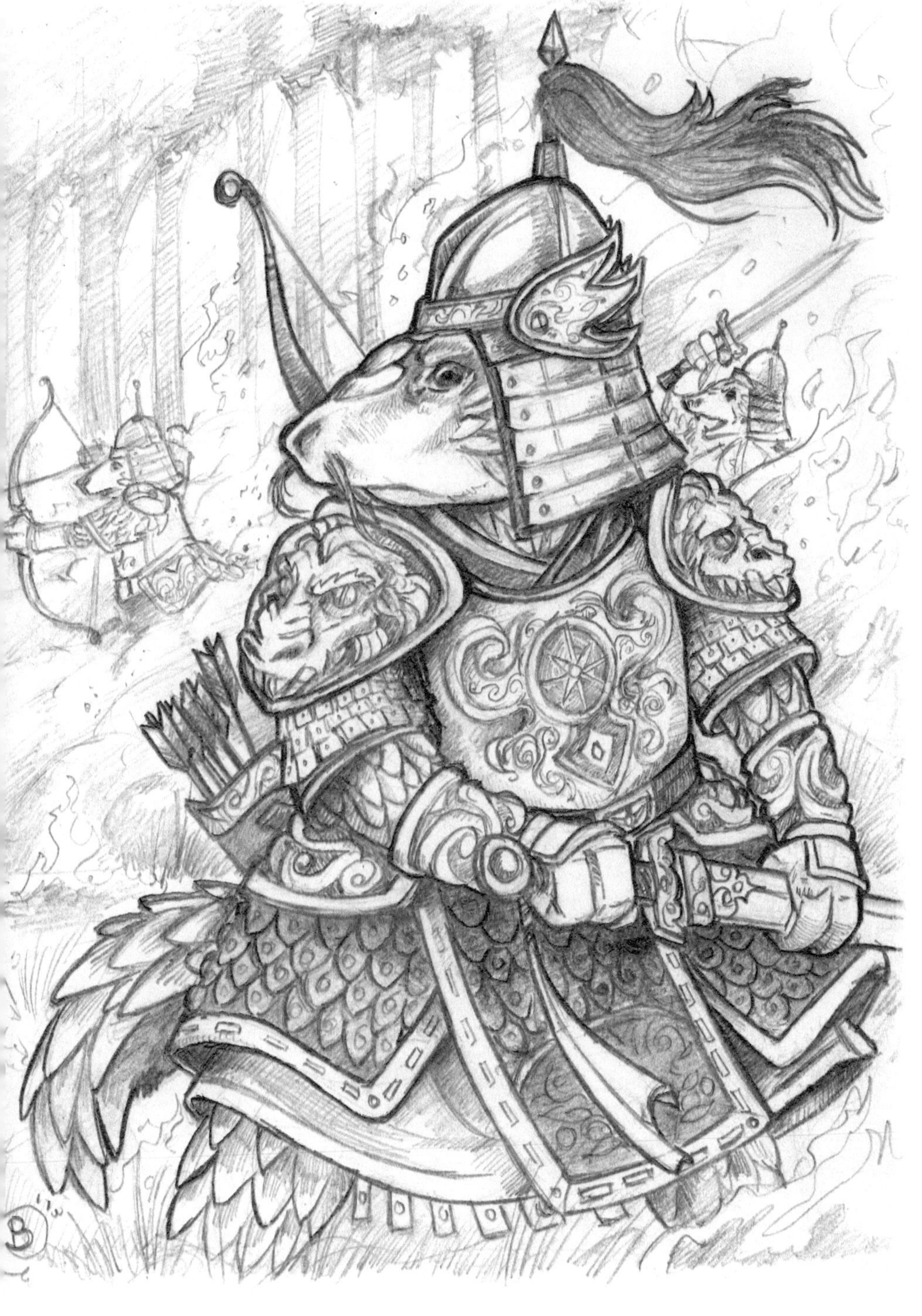

Lucky Lo

Captain of the Cat's Whiskers

Louisa MacClau is the third captain to hold the name Lucky Lo and by far the most successful. Her predecessors were beset with horrible fortune on the high seas; Lothar Hanson was hit by a cannonball at the battle of Butcher's Bay and Louis Finch was made to walk the plank by his own men. Louisa, however, has a knack for crew management and cutthroat skullduggery. She's a multi-tasker.

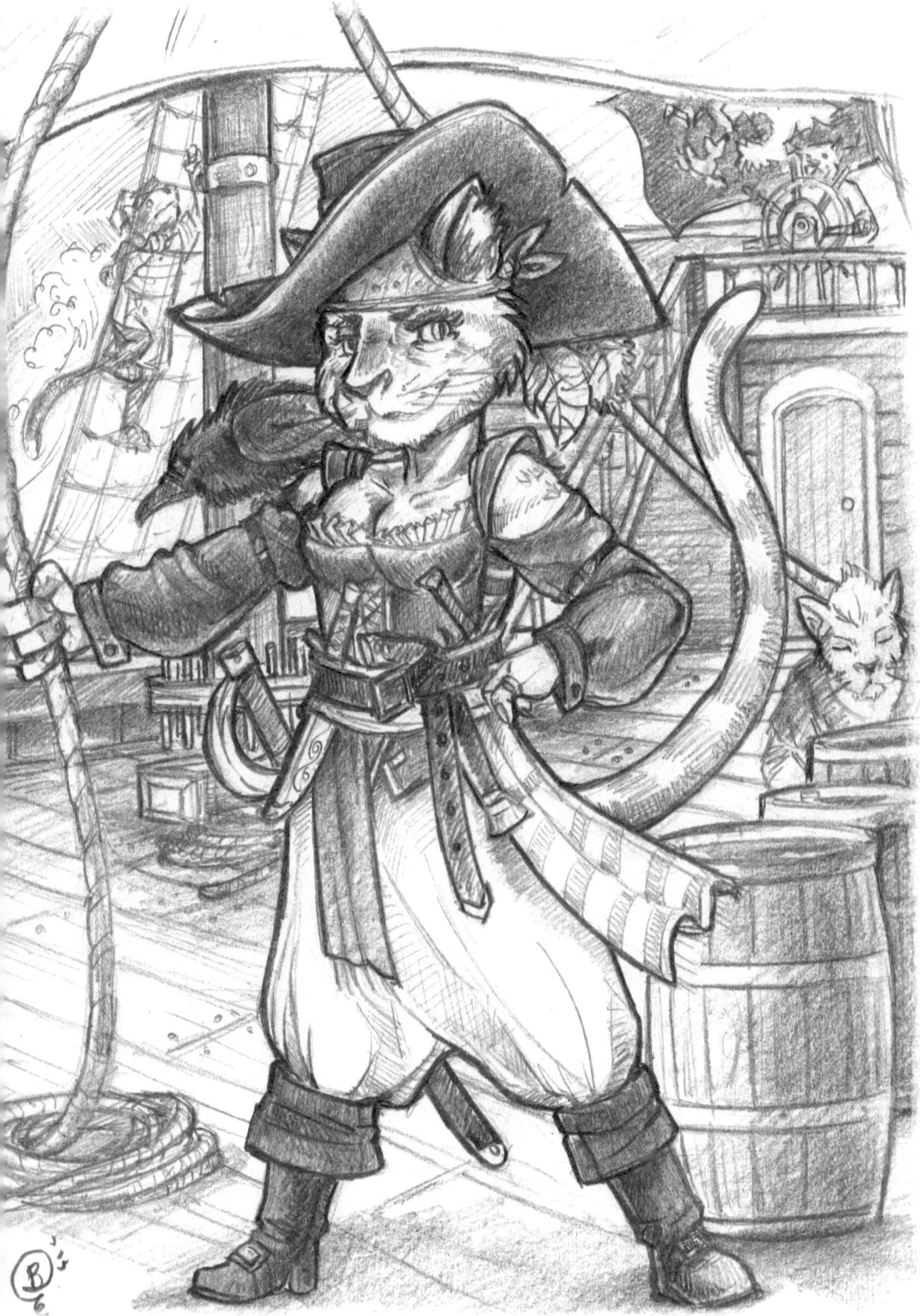

Maester Rykenhirsch

The White Stag

The Library of High Arcanum is one of the greatest treasures of all time, and the keeper of this knowledge trove is an equally formidable being. Rykenhirsch, also known as The White Stag, is the protector of millennia of magical research and discovery. He doesn't remember his mortal life before he became a lich in service to the library, but he's said whatever he lost in exchange for knowledge was well worth the trade.

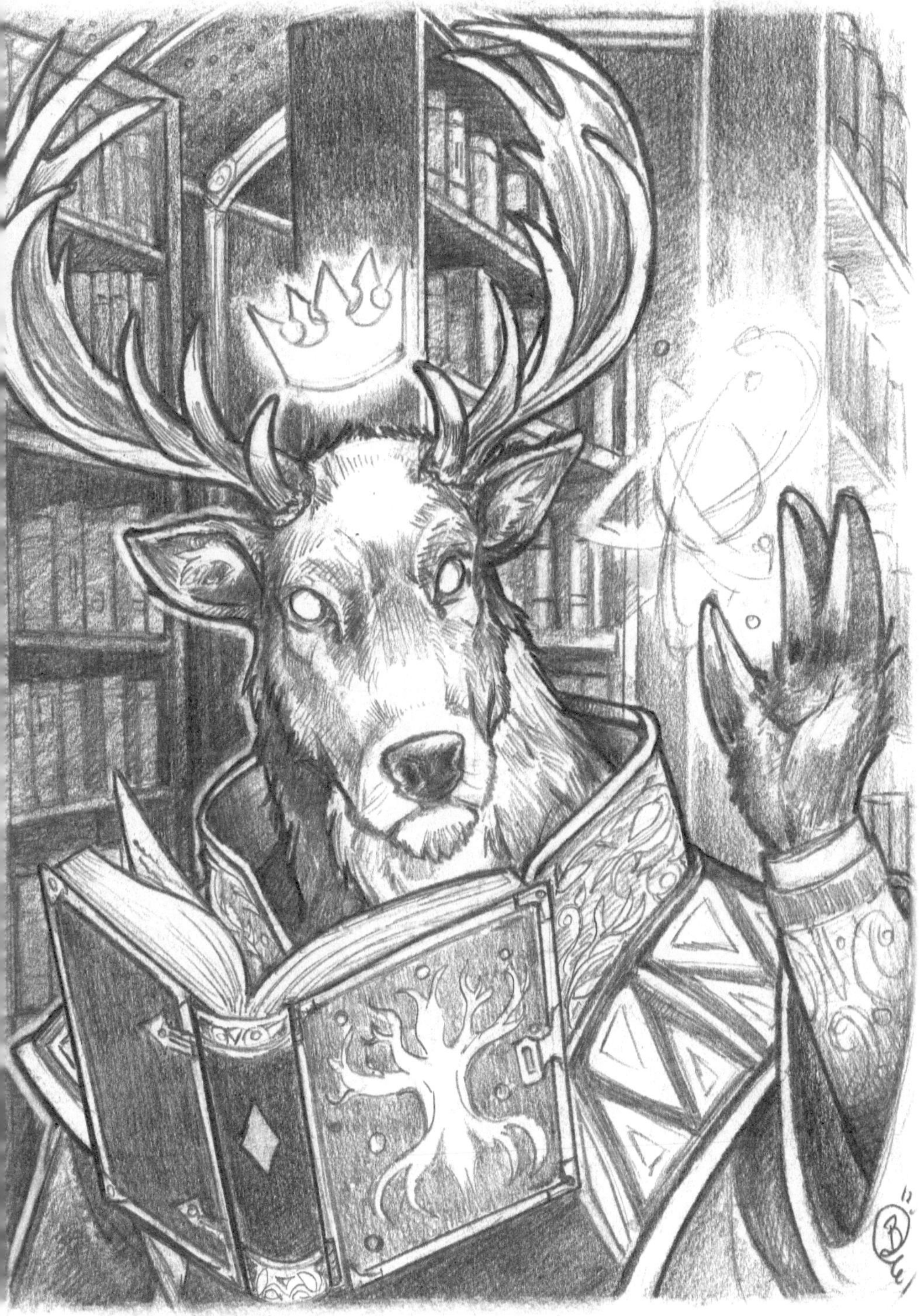

Angus Ellington Smythe

Owner and Proprietor of The Warren

Come, seekers and adventurers! Visit the finest tavern in the Woodland - The Warren! Here you'll find dungeon divers rubbing elbows with soldiers of fortune. Trade tales of peril and intrigue over a fine mug of ale, or just get in a rousing fistfight with fellow brawlers. Angus E. Smythe, your humble host, has never met a beast he didn't like, and never turns away good money.

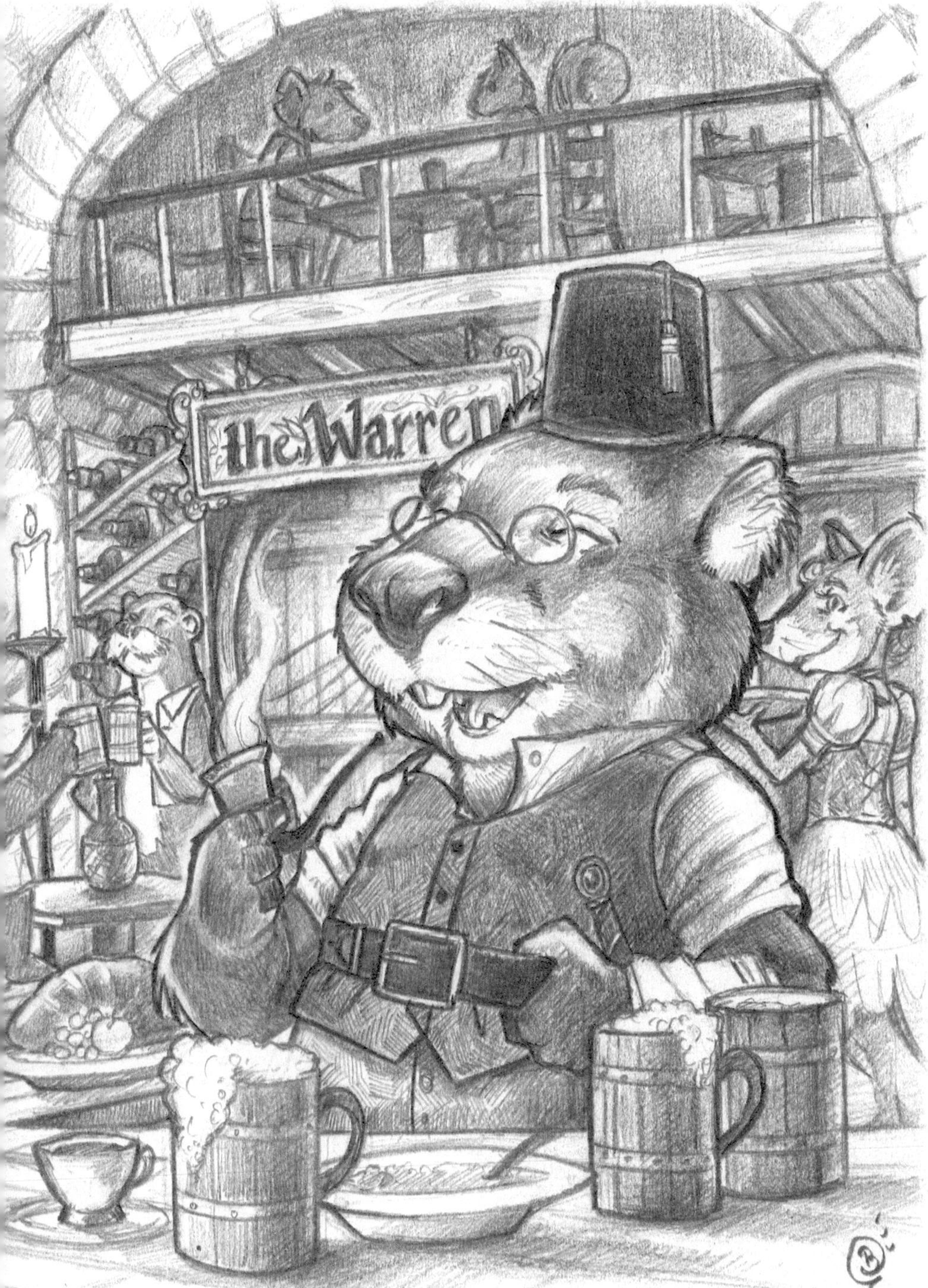

Salah Almasafir

The Traveler

In the east lies the Kal-Immishi Dessert, also called The Sea of Long Journeys. It is a harsh and desolate land, battered by the sun and wind and the final resting place of many wayward souls. Few try to cross it, but those that do face death with each step into endless sands. A guide is a necessity, and Salah Almasafir is the best there is. He knows every trail, every ruin, and every oasis from the Casma Flats to the Towers of Othar - and he's never lost a traveler to the desert.

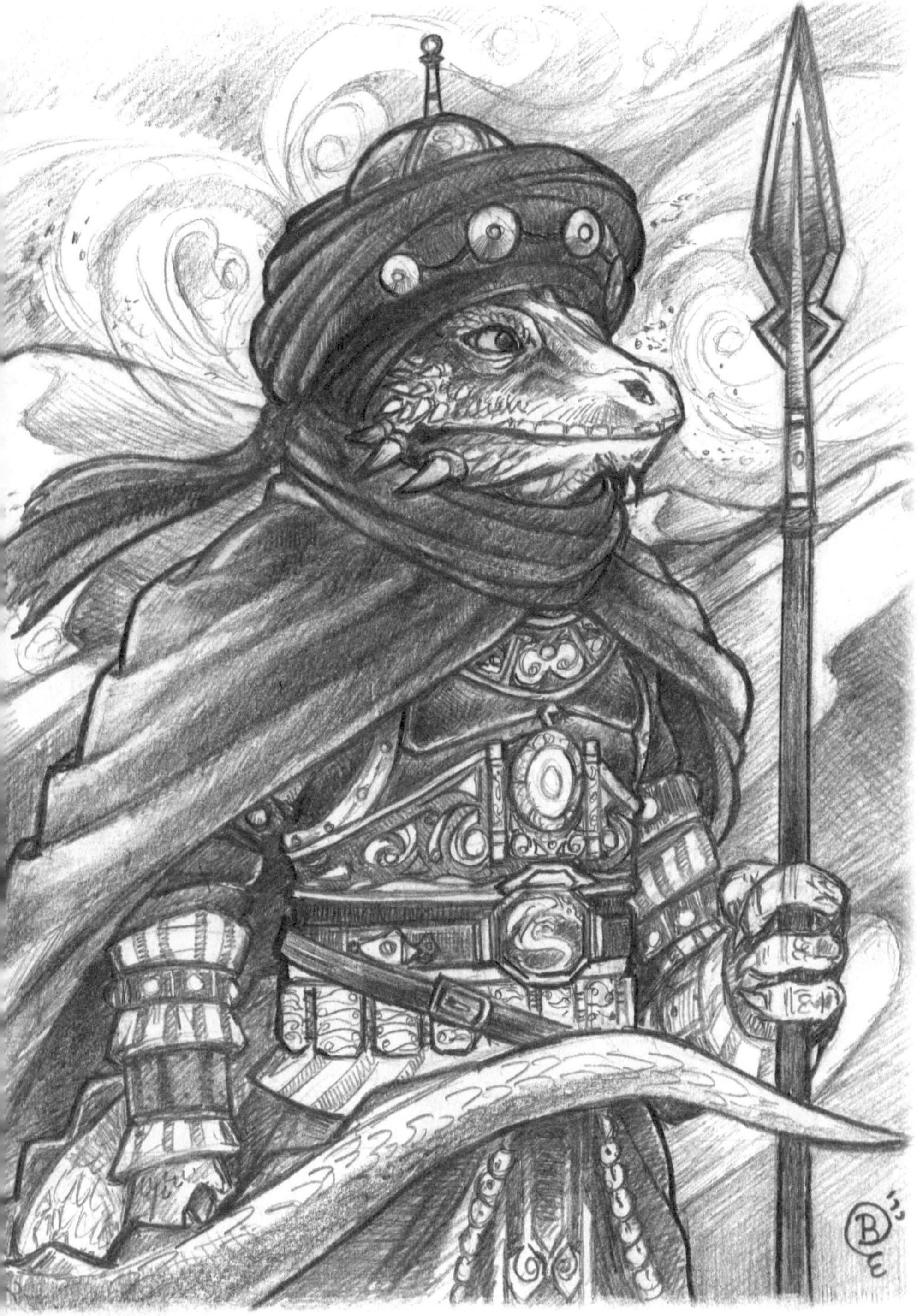

Aiko

Ninja of the Three-Tailed Clan

"Beware the blades of the Three-Tailed Clan." Aiko heard those words many times in her village as a child. They were the monsters under the bed, the darkest shadows in your nightmares, but when the soldiers came and took her father, Aiko knew they were her only hope. She called on them to save him, and their price was set; Aiko's lifelong allegiance. It was a price she was happy to pay.

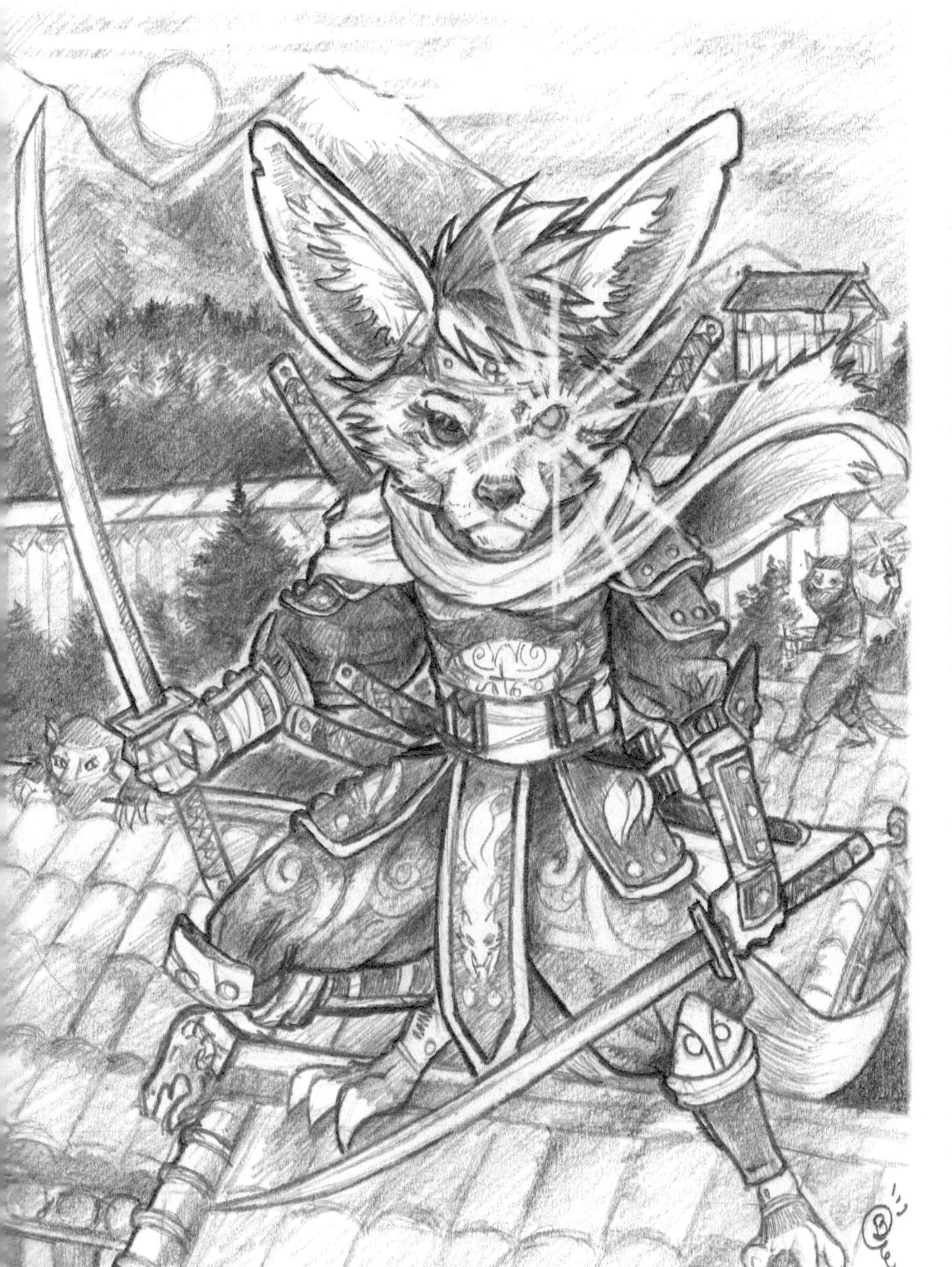

Mother Ursahlia

Druid of Aurora

The Druids of Aurora serve the Light of Lights, and Ursahlia is their highest cleric. As such, she is gifted with the divine light, but don't let her good nature fool you. She has known loss and pain, and it has made her strong. Her powers give the ability to heal, but she is also trained in varied forms of hand to hand combat. When evil comes to her forest, nothing is as dangerous as this mother bear.

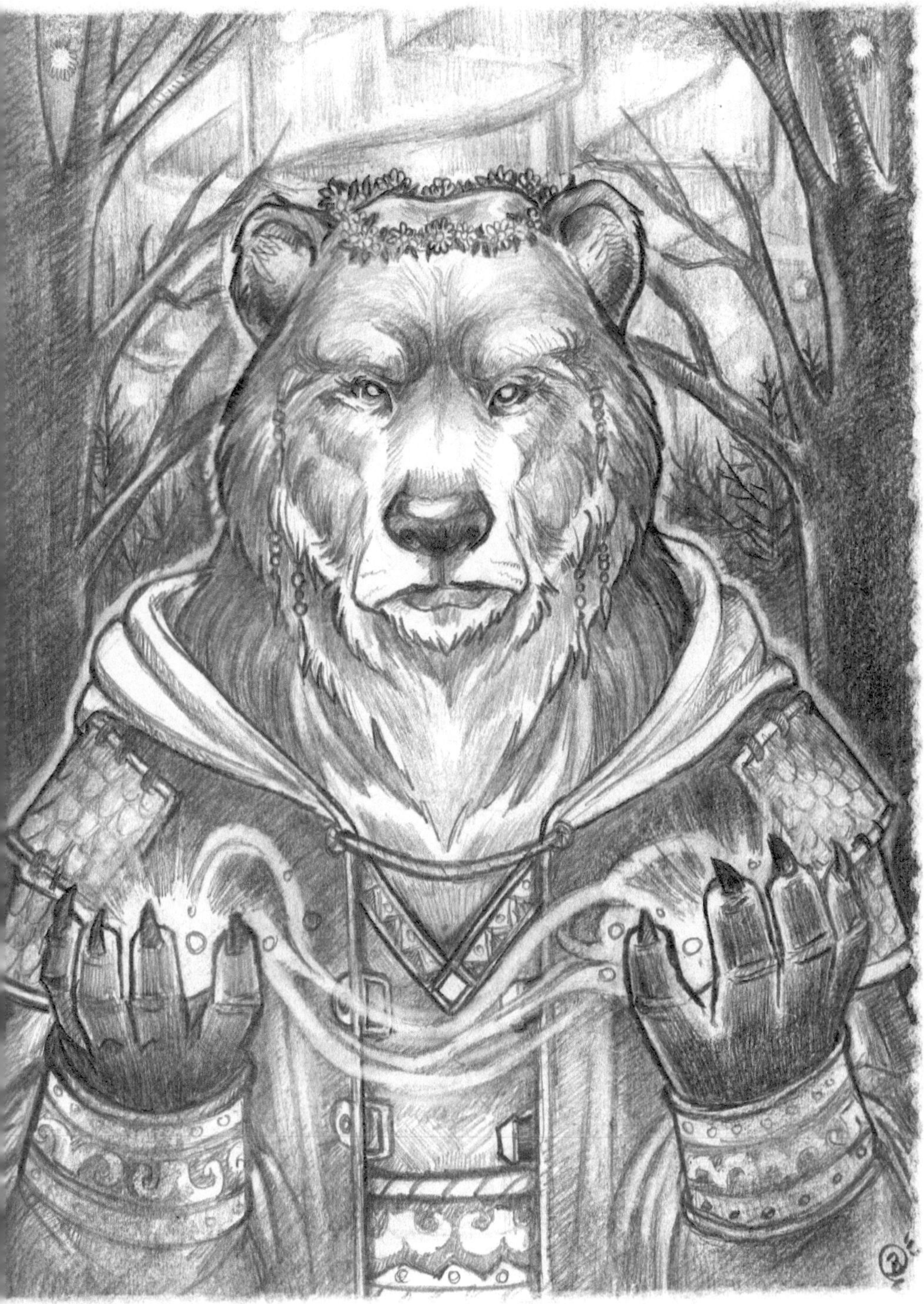

Rochiel Redleaf

Woodland Warden

Rochiel and her comrades are legendary in the Wood-lands. They're called the Wardens - guardians of the borderlands. They are the first line of defense against the Skulking Horde. From the light dappled canopy, they wait invisibly for their foes, ready to rain down arrows on any beast that would do harm to the Woodland Folk.

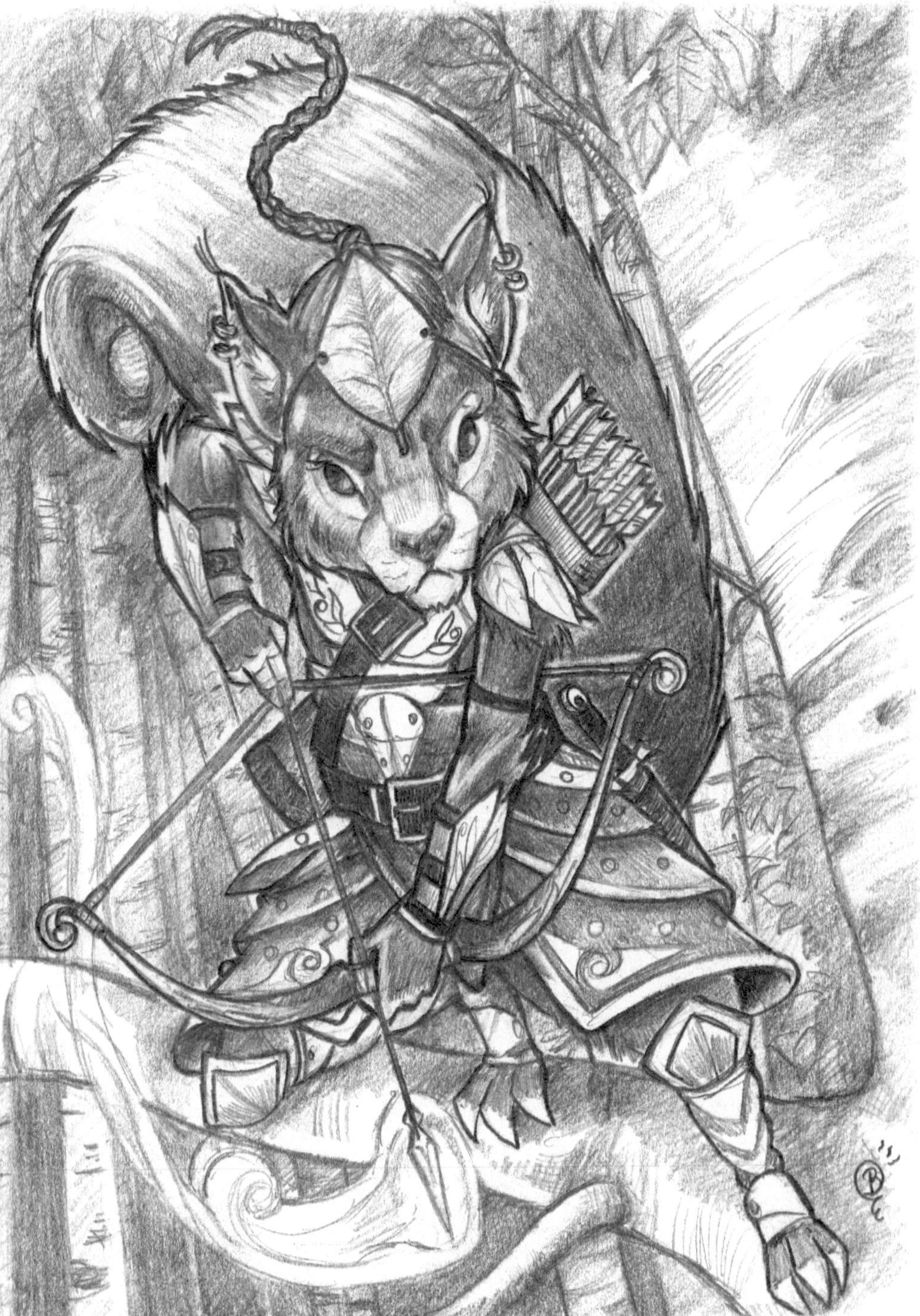

Beauford A. Fontenot

Gentleman Bog Wizard

The wetlands hold a special power all their own - a kind of lilting song that hangs in the air like early morning mist. The trained ear of a bog wizard can hear magic in that song. Beauford has spent the better part of his life learning the secrets of this natural power and harnessing it to his will. Now there is no spell, no incantation, and no spirit that is beyond this young toad's grasp.

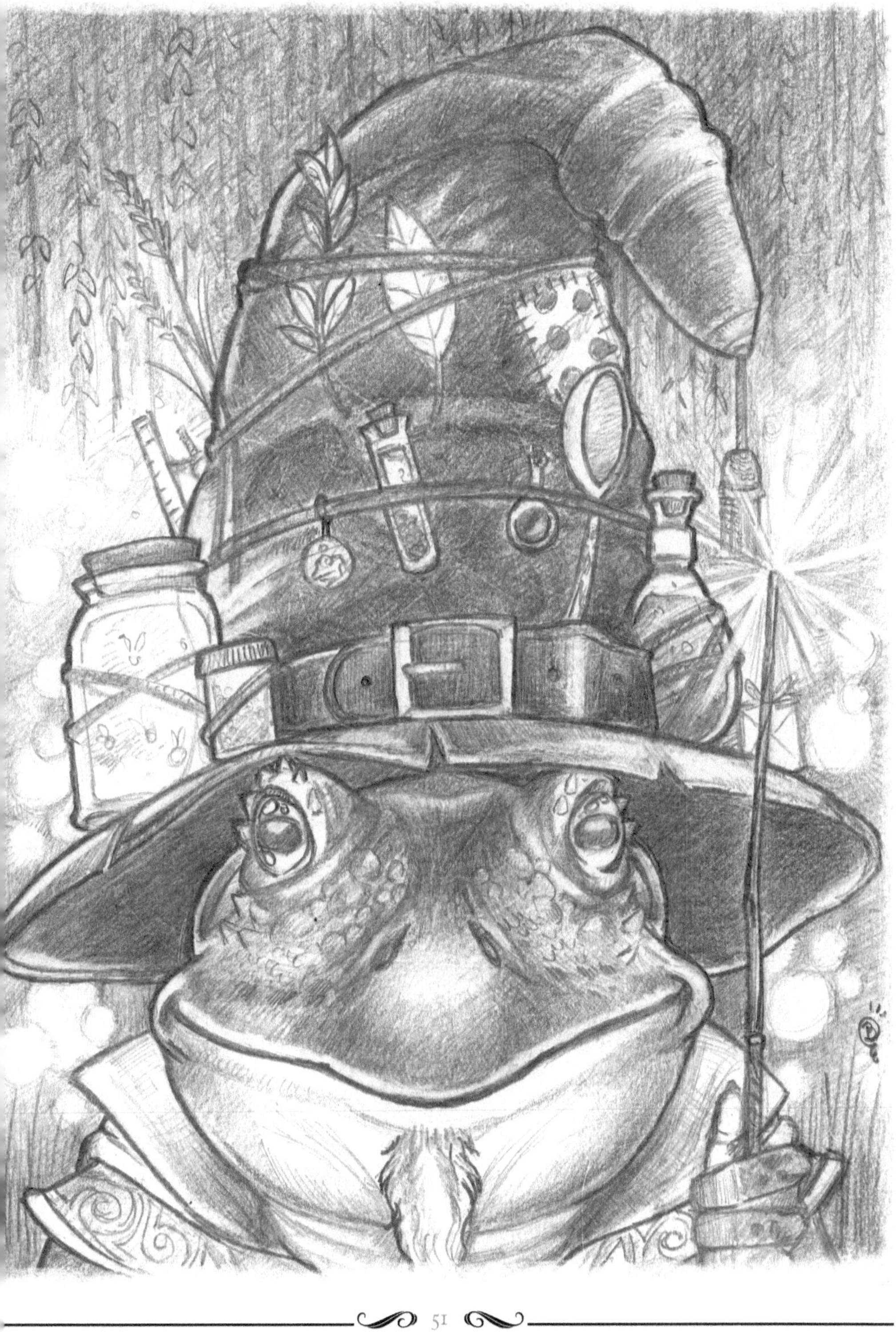

Braeden Mael Mochan

The River Monk

Braeden follows The Way of the Salmon - a form of fighting that finds its inspiration in the streams and rivers of his homeland. The fluid movements of this ancient art are quick and fierce, and when used by a master river monk, are a dance of arcane force unlike any ever seen. He becomes one with the water around him and an instrument of its natural strength.

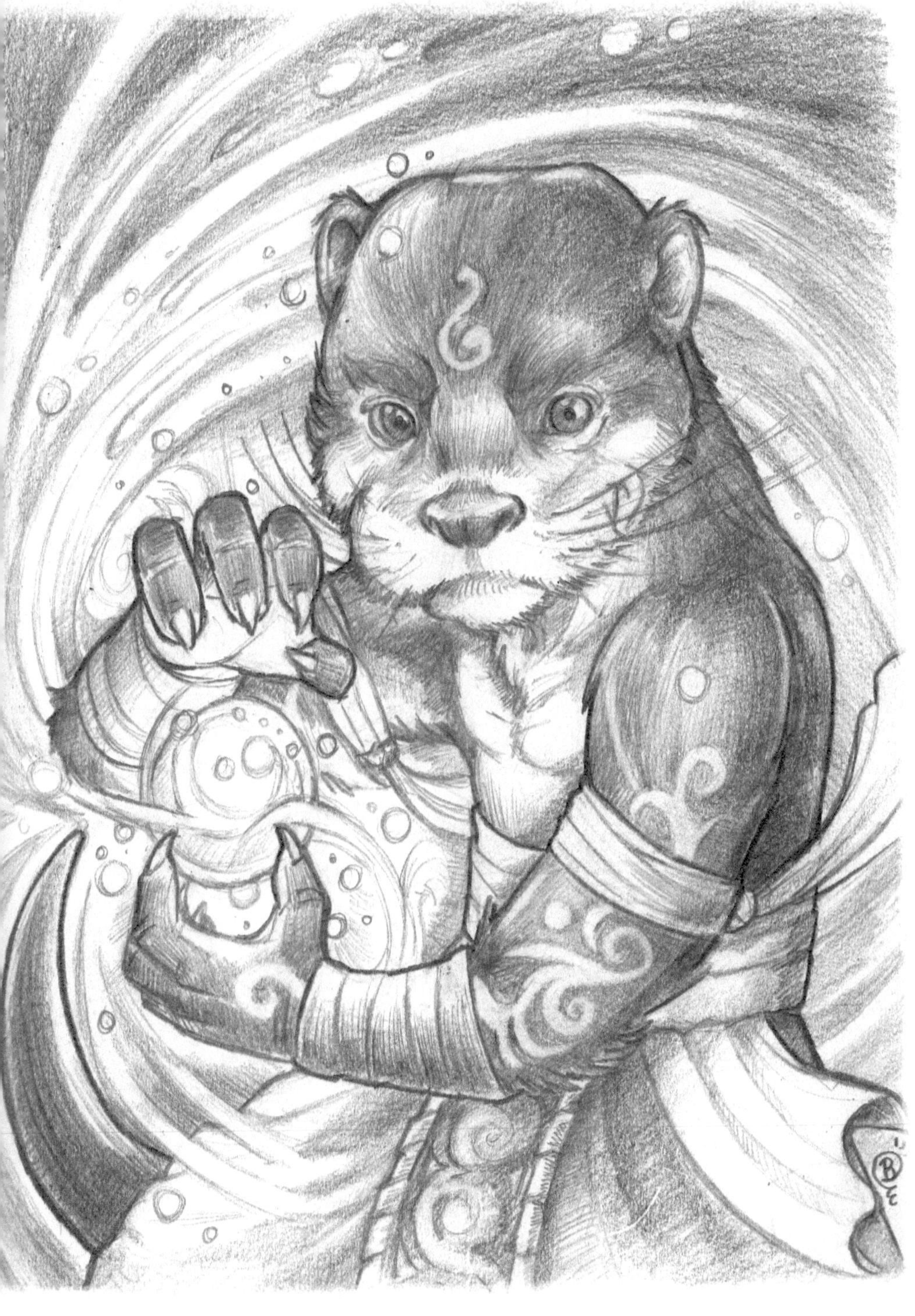

Captain Jaeger Von Reinhardt

City Guard of Kriegerburg

Kriegerburg is called "The Soldier City," and with good reason. It stands at the gateway to the Eastern Sea, a land filled with pirates and brigands of all kinds. It is the last bastion of order before the lawless coast. Capt. Reinhardt knows the danger facing him and his men every day, and he relishes a good fight. The city guard is a well-oiled weapon, ready to be drawn at a moments notice.

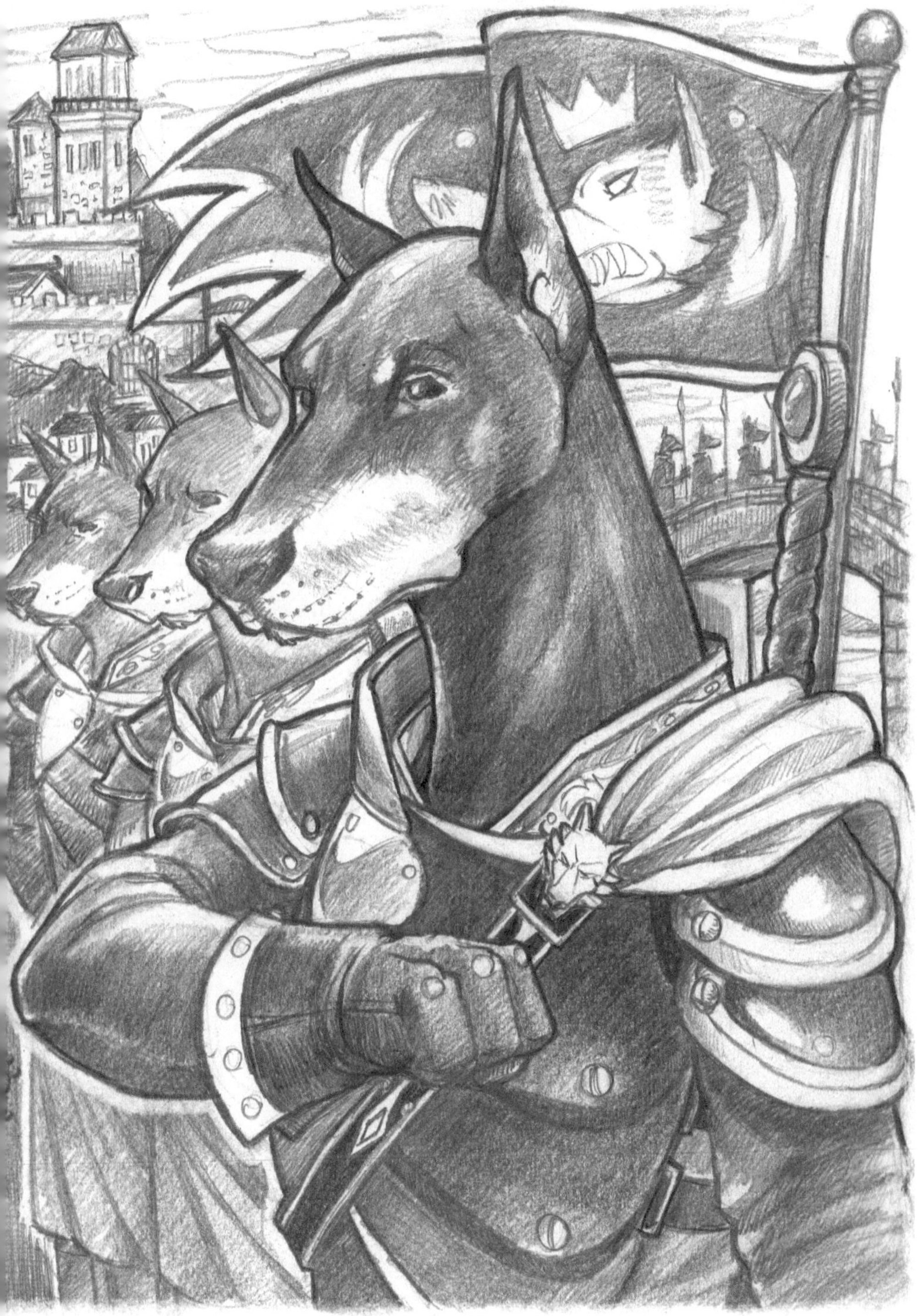

Otto Platinus

Professional Dungeon Diver

It's hard to imagine anyone with worse luck than poor ole' Otto. His job takes him to some pretty terrible places, and he's been chased by everything from undead skeletons to carnivorous shadow beasts. Sadly, the loot he finds is never that valuable. His sweet wife, Petunia, wishes he'd take a safer job, but Otto holds out hope that the big score he's been searching for is right around the next dangerous corner.

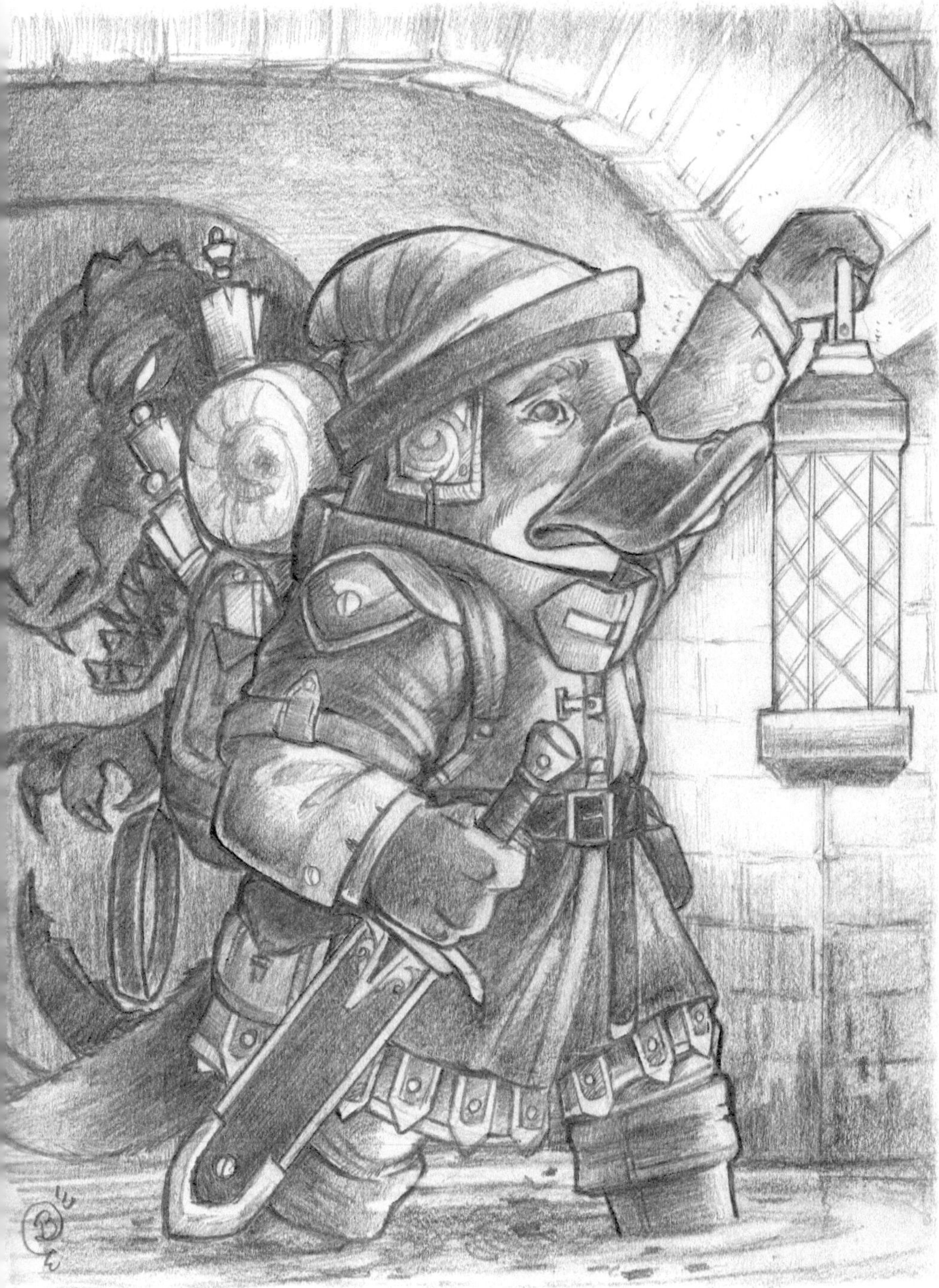

Kal Ish Udama

The Golden Mage

Little is known about the Golden Mage, and that is just the way he likes it. He guides adventurers, thwarts evil, and discovers secrets that have lain hidden for centuries. The effect of his influence has been felt throughout the four kingdoms for over 400 years, but he prefers to be like the wind - powerful, ever-present, and unseen.

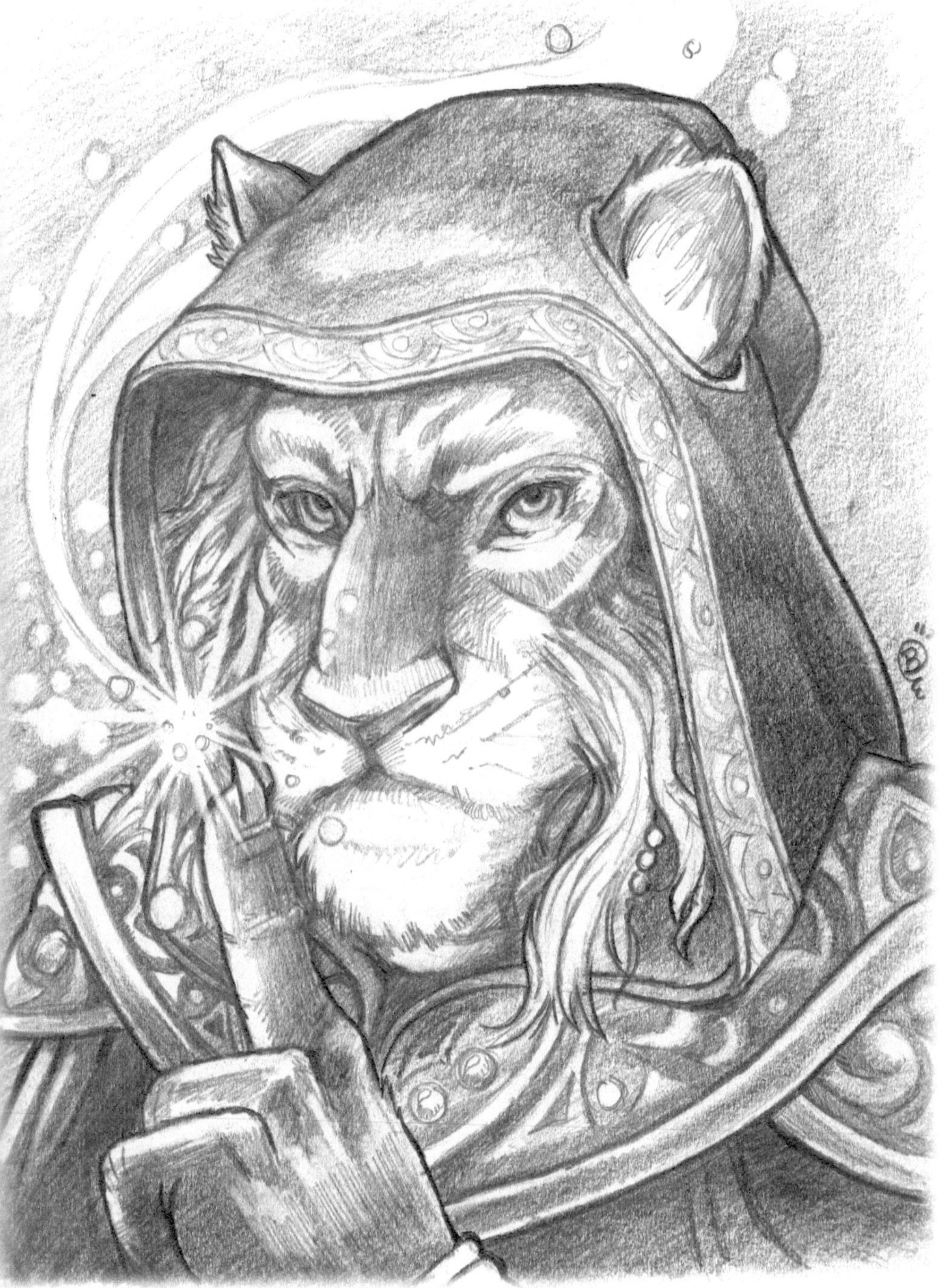

Taleisan

The Bard

Famous for his lengthy odes and epics, Taleisan travels the Woodlands to bring the joy of music to the village folk and the Skulking Horde as well. Under that jovial smile and charming facade lies a calculating mind - the mind of a spy. Taleisan has the advantage of being welcomed by both the vile and virtuous, and he uses that advantage to trade in the most valuable of commodities - information.

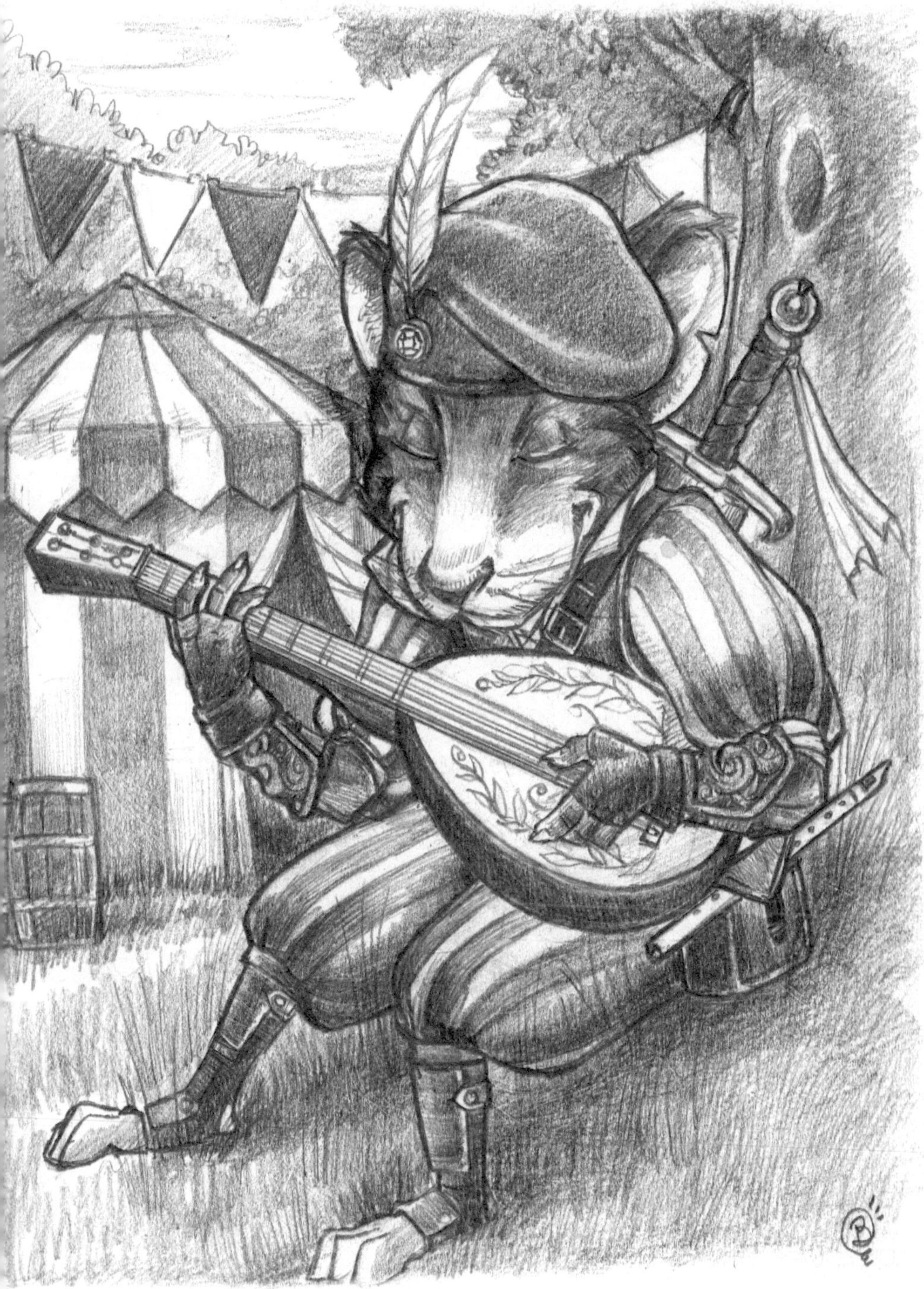

Katerina the Giving

The Hedge Witch

The Ishtar Cauldron was given to the children of Yaga the Wise generations ago and passed from mother to daughter down through the ages. Katerina the Giving is the last in a long line of gifted witches, using her powers to help the people of the Woodland. During the long winters, any beast in need can rely on her for food or aid. Her vegetable stew is famous, so warm and rejuvenating that it's almost magic.

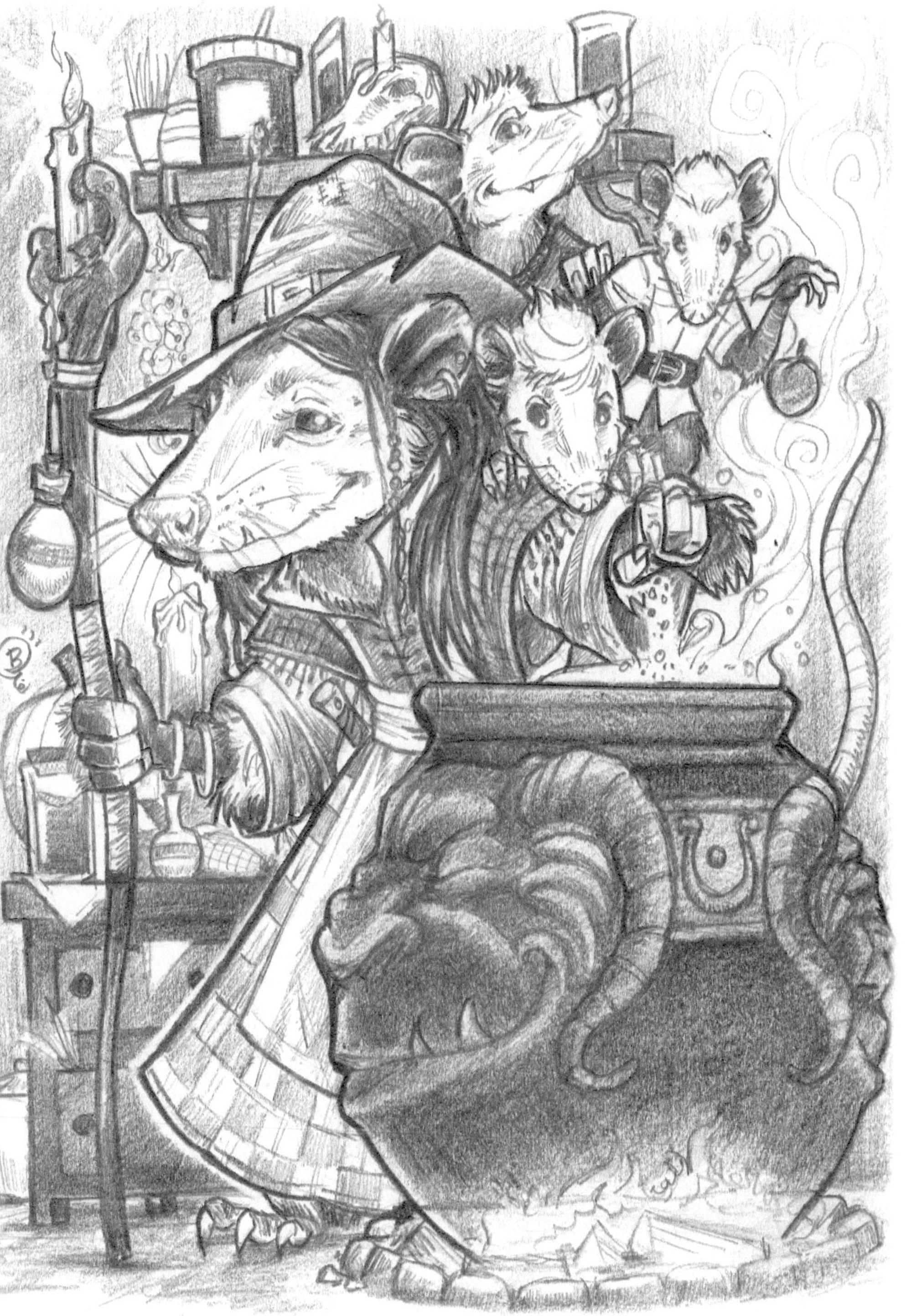

Faldspar

Keeper of Umber's Throne

A millennia ago, dragons were worshipped as gods in the four kingdoms, but no more. The greatest among them, Umber the Sacred, was struck down from his throne by an even higher power. Since that day, dragons have not been able to fly - penance for reaching too high. A prophecy tells that a true and noble dragon will one day sit in Umber's place, lifting the curse on his people. Some still have faith in that redemption, and Faldspar keeps the throne of Umber safe in hopes that his people may ascend to the heavens once more.

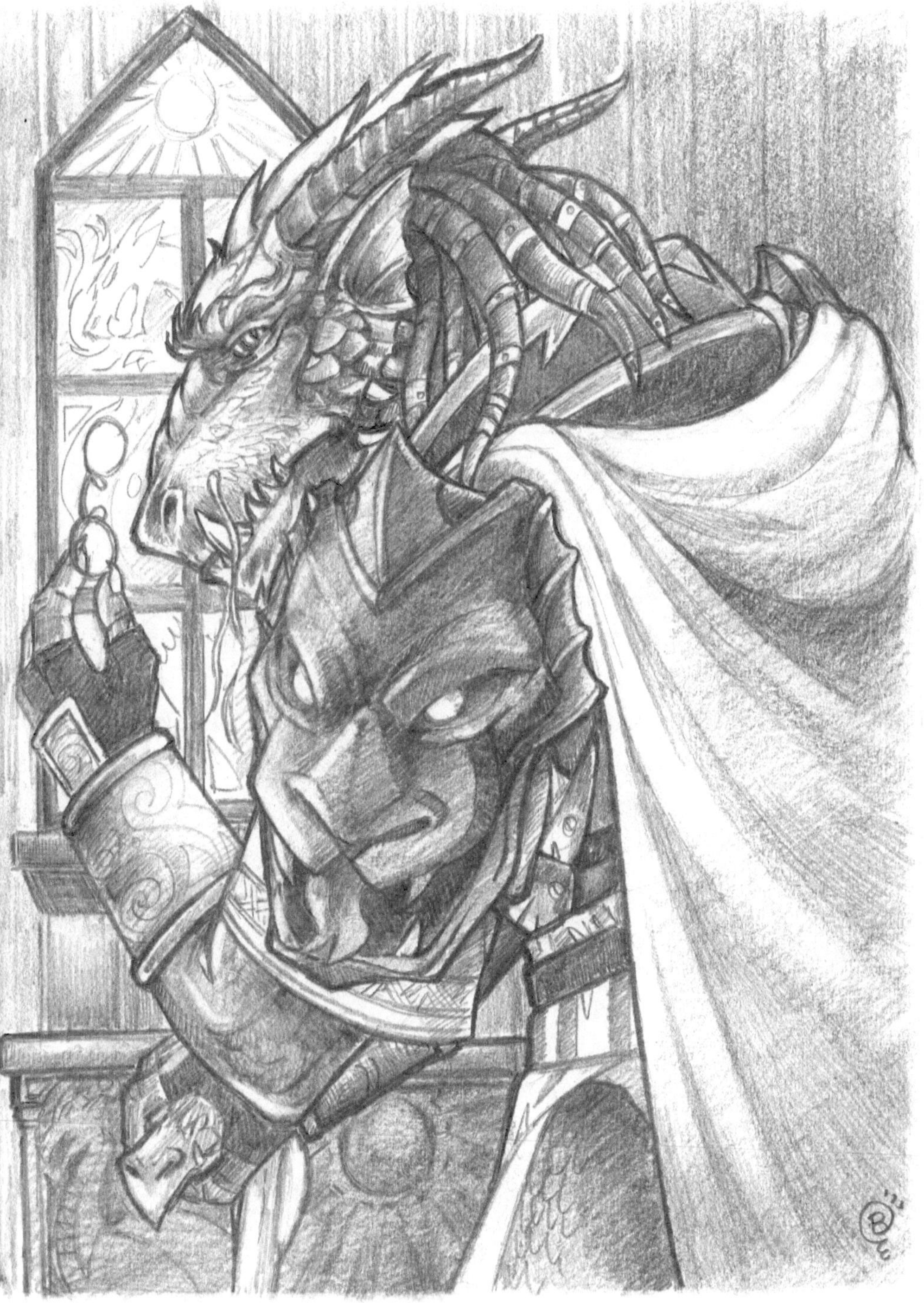

Aquias Griffe

The Boss of Bosses

There is a den, deep in the Woodland, where only the bravest of beasts go. It is a place of secrets, deception, and dastardly deals. Underworld figures gather there to kiss the ring of the Boss of Bosses, the Prince of Cutpurses, the Godfather of the Wood - Aquias Griffe. You'll find him there, sitting at his oaken table with a cup of fine tea, sharpening his claws. Be careful what you ask of him - he never forgets a debt.

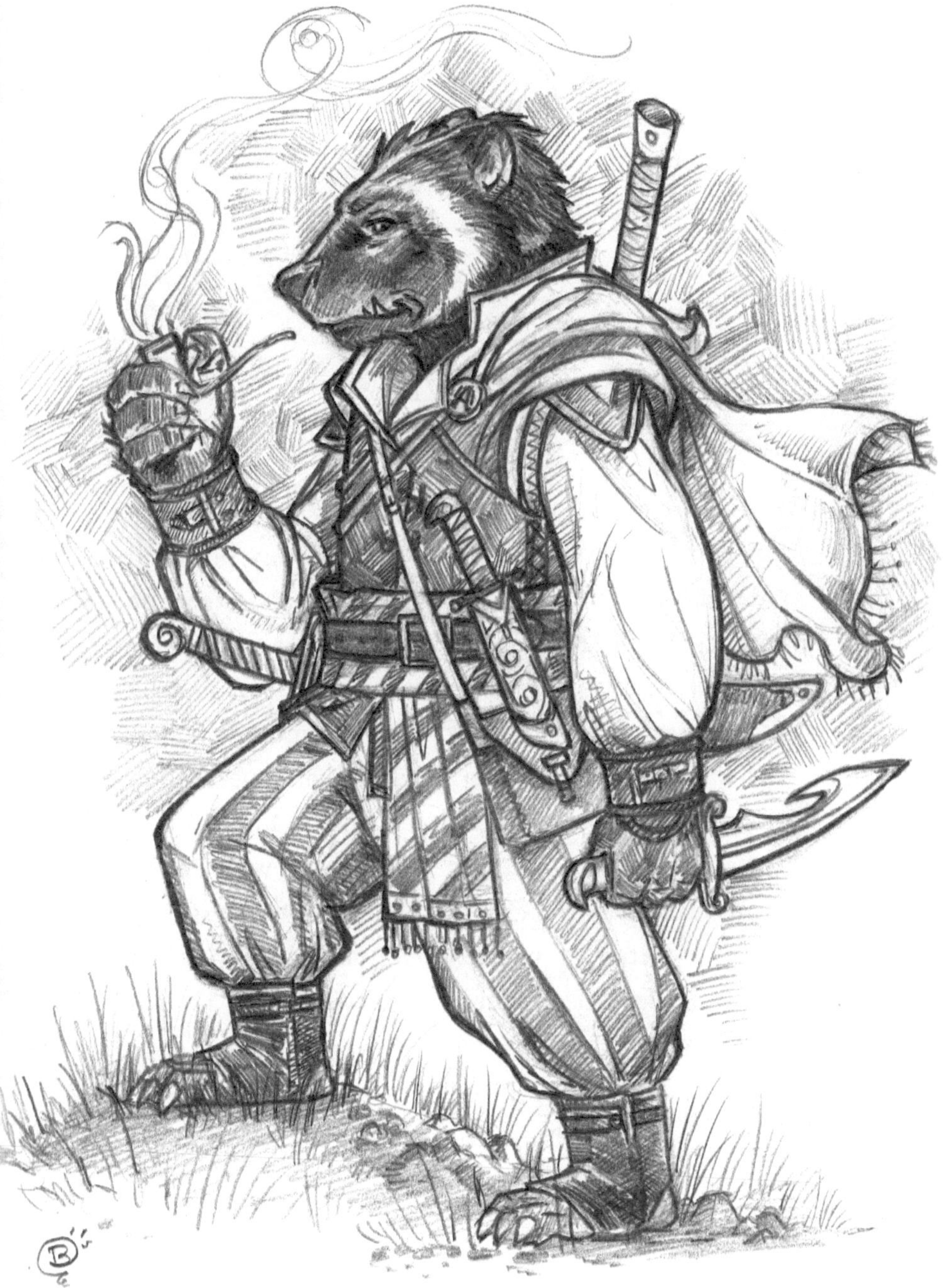

inspired by Kyle Sullivan

Rashad Ibn Abas

Great Lion of the Sea

Warrior. Scholar. King. Rashad trekked across the Kal-Immishi Dessert when he was just a boy, traveling with traders and silk merchants, all for the chance to see the Library of High Arcanum in Albasur. The ancient center of learning sat on the glistening eastern coast, but by the time Rashad reached the city it was almost in flames. War had come to Albasur, and Rashad was drafted into service. In battle he proved himself, and through his knowledge and virtue he gained the respect of all he met. He saved the city, and when the war was over Rashad Ibn Abas was named king. And what was his first decree? To be left alone for a week in the library. He *had* fought a war to see it after all.

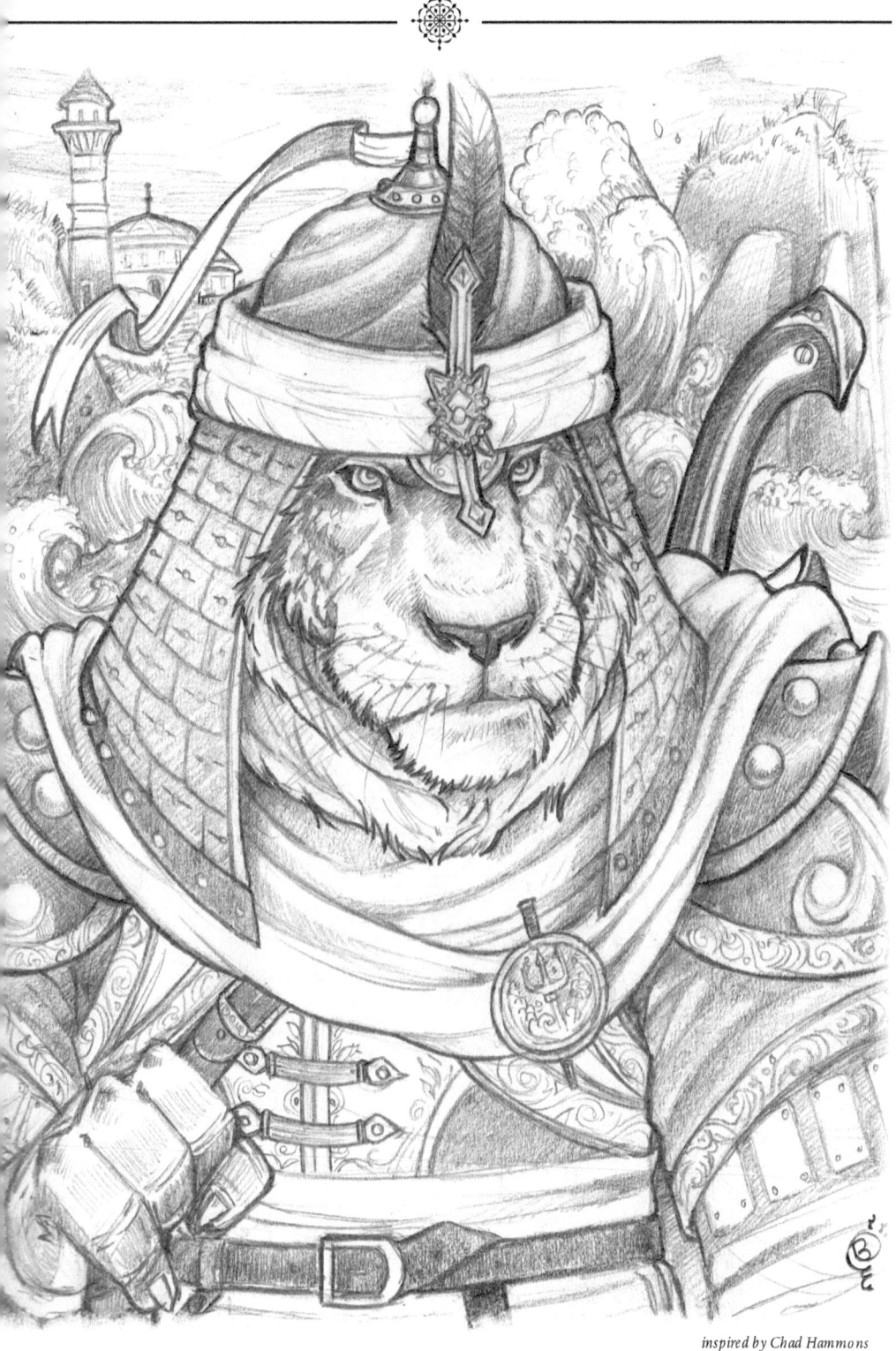

inspired by Chad Hammons

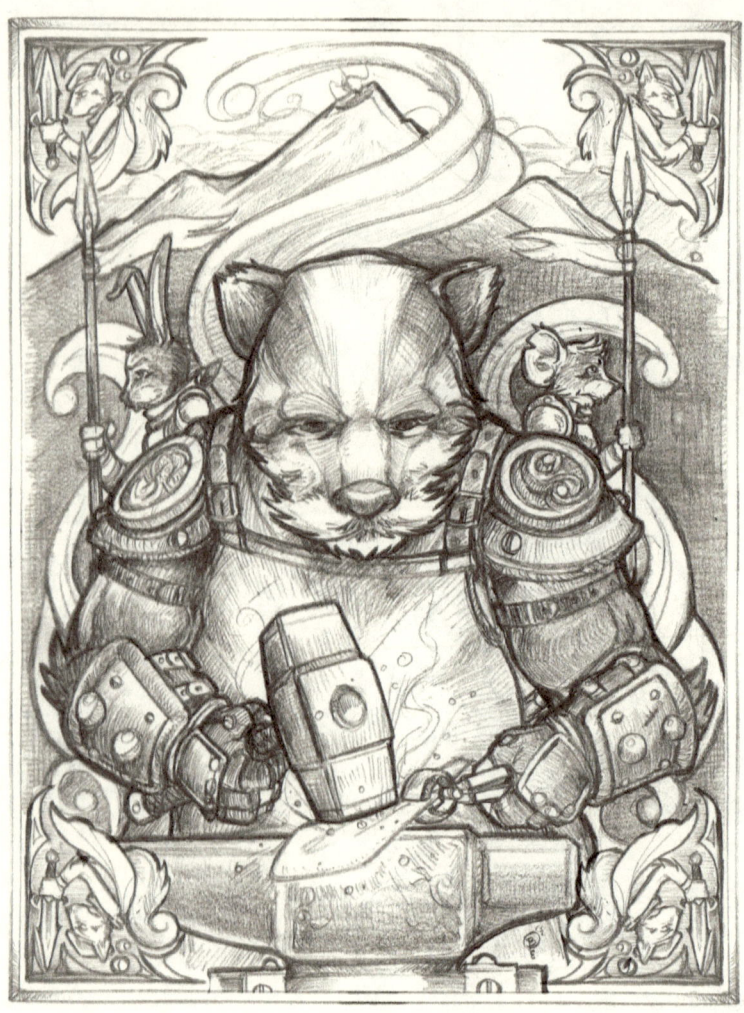

Brian W. Parker
Author, Illustrator, and Creator of the Fantastical

Brian grew up in Alaska, then Mississippi, and has always been in love with storytelling in every medium. He earned a BFA in graphic design & illustration and an MA in writing & publishing. Brian now spends his days working in youth publishing (so cool, right?) through his company, Believe In Wonder, which he co-owns with his wife, Josie. He is the author of *Crow in the Hollow, You Can Rely on Platypi*, and co-author of *Obi The Changeling, Nicholas & Sabina in The Busy Season* and *The Wonderous Science*

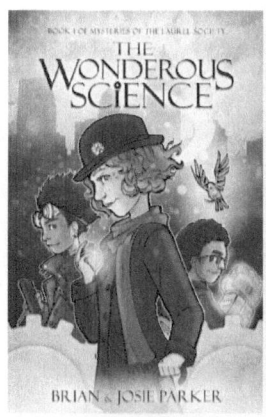
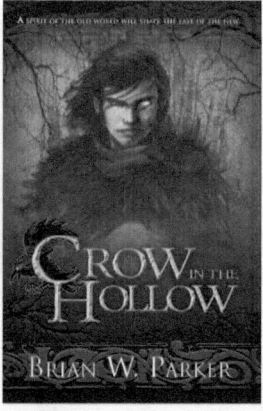
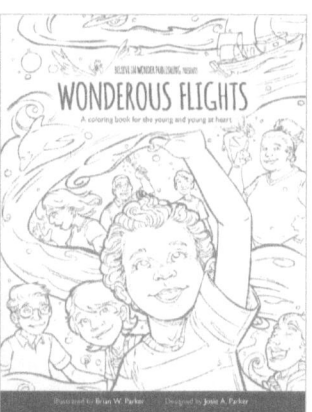
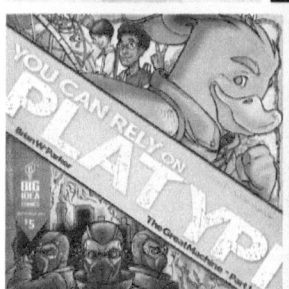
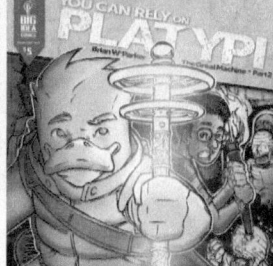
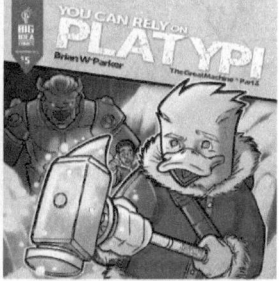
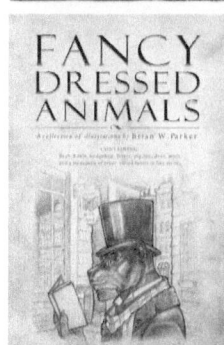
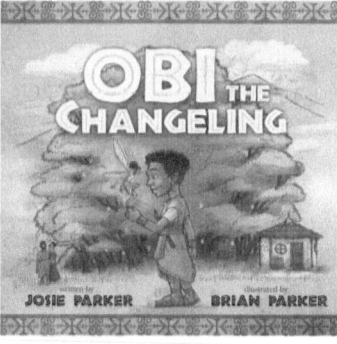
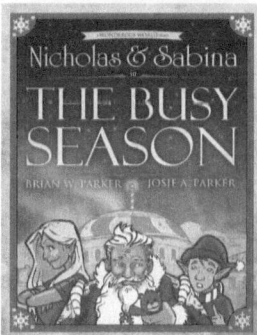

www.ingramcontent.com/pod-product-compliance
Lightning Source LLC
Chambersburg PA
CBHW020613220526
45463CB00006B/2574